International Vegetarian Cooking

International Vegetarian Cooking

—◆—

Judy Ridgway

THE CROSSING PRESS
FREEDOM, CALIFORNIA

Identification of Photographs following page 84

Photo A	Garlic Sauce with Vegetables (page 172) and Tapenade with toasted bread (page 170)
Photo B	Vegetable Terrine (page 154)
Photo C	Spaghetti with Walnut, Parsley, and Basil Sauce (page 50)
Photo D	Garlic Mushrooms (pages 26-27)
Photo E	Vegetable Tagine (page 69)
Photo F	Fettucini with Sautéed Spring Vegetables (page 45), Chinese Money Bags (page 163), and Fresh Ratatouille (page 83) on a bed of bulgur wheat
Photo G	Mixed Vegetables with Sunflower Seed Dumplings (page 100)
Photo H	Chive and Tomato Soufflé (page 109)

CONTENTS

———◆———

Introduction

Vegetarian food is both enjoyable and nutritious. The inspiration for the recipes in this everyday cookbook came from all the major cuisines of the world. There are soups, casseroles, and pies in the Northern European tradition; curries, dhals, and stir-fries from the Far East; and specialties like couscous and falafel from North Africa and the Middle East. Even more important, perhaps, is the influence of the "Mediterranean diet," with its reliance on olive oil, garlic, fresh vegetables, beans, and pasta. This diet is now thought to be the healthiest in the world.

Cooking is an art that really needs time, but how many of us home cooks can spend more than an hour or so in the kitchen? Indeed, even that amount of time often seems too long to take from the many other demands of the day. Quick pasta or rice dishes and stir-fries are the modern answer, and I have included plenty of these.

The recipes are based on fresh produce and whole grains rather than processed foods out of cans and packages. My exceptions to the use of unprocessed foods include canned tomatoes, frozen peas, and frozen spinach. You will need at least twice as much fresh spinach as frozen, possibly even three times the amount. There are a couple of recipes that do require fresh, not frozen, spinach, and I have indicated when this is so.

I have also used canned beans throughout. For me the convenience value outweighs any slight loss in vitamin content. This can be made up in extra fresh fruit and vegetables. (If you want to use dried beans, see page x.)

Whole-grain products are, I believe, the best, but sometimes a more attractive result is achieved by using more processed products. I leave the choice to you, stating in the recipe whether a specific type of ingredient is easier to work with.

NUTRITION

The most generally accepted guidelines for healthy eating suggest that we should:

1. Eat less fat.

We should confine our fat intake to 33 percent of our total calories. The World Health Organization (WHO) recommendations go even further and set the figure at 30 percent.

For the average sedentary adult now consuming 38 percent of total energy as fats, this means a reduction in daily intake of about 1 ounce per day. In food terms this is about 2 tablespoons of oil or a matchbox-sized amount of solid fat. The fat eaten should be composed mainly of polyunsaturated and monounsaturated fatty acids.

These guidelines, which are based on the growing conviction that fat and particularly saturated fat plays a major part in the incidence of coronary heart disease, are not very difficult for the vegetarian to encompass. After all, saturated fats are mainly found in animal products, and mono- and polyunsaturated fats are found mainly in vegetable oil.

However, saturated fats *are* found in dairy products such as milk, butter, and cheese, and lacto-vegetarians do need to watch the amount of such foods that they eat. Saturated fats are also found in chocolate and, in the form of palm and coconut oil, in some cakes and cookies, so check the ingredients listed on the label, or make your own.

Research into the effects of different kinds of fatty acids on the incidence of coronary heart disease indicates that both polyunsaturated fats such as corn and sunflower oil, and monounsaturated fats like olive and avocado oil have a beneficial effect on the cholesterol content of the blood.

The WHO recommendations set an upper limit of 7 percent of energy on polyunsaturated fats but no upper limit on monounsaturates. However, a good deal more research is required before we can decide what proportions of each would be more beneficial. In the meantime, I personally opt for a mix of polyunsaturated margarine for spreading on bread, and monounsaturated olive oil for cooking, flavoring, and dressings. Olive oil is specified in a recipe if it is important for the flavor of the finished dish; otherwise, I just say "vegetable oil" and leave the choice to you. When using olive oil, extra-virgin olive oil has the most flavor.

2. Eat more cereals and starchy foods.

This is necessary to make up the calorie loss from eating less fat. Most vegetarians will choose to eat whole-grain cereals, and these products tend to be more nutritious because there is often a substantial loss of vitamins in refined cereals.

3. Eat more dietary fiber.

Fiber also has a part to play in the prevention of heart disease, as well as diseases of the digestive tract and varicose veins. Eating whole-grain cereals, such as oats and brown rice, and whole-wheat bread helps to increase the fiber content of the diet. Lentils, dried beans, and peas, and fresh fruit and vegetables also add to the total.

4. Eat less sugar and salt.

These recommendations are more controversial. The former is based on the fact that sugar intake plays a part in tooth decay and possibly overeating. The arguments against salt are based on the suggestion that high salt intake is associated with high blood pressure. This is probably true for some sections of the population, but at present scientists are unable to predict exactly who is at risk of developing high blood pressure.

5. Think about vitamin and mineral intake.

Iron is an important consideration for the vegetarian, as the richest sources are animal-based. Other sources include bread and breakfast cereals, dried apricots, potatoes, and leafy vegetables, especially the cabbage family and watercress. Eating a vitamin C-rich food at the same meal can double the absorption of iron, so orange juice with toast or black currants with muesli are good combinations.

The vitamin B group, particularly B_6, folic acid, and B_{12}, is also important. Folic acid, found in leafy green vegetables, works with vitamin B_{12} in the formation of red blood cells. However, like many other vitamins it is highly unstable and can be affected by cooking and long storage.

To make the most of any vitamin source, the food must be eaten when it is as fresh as possible, and a few nutritionists go so far as to advocate eating at least one meal of raw fresh food every day.

PRACTICALITIES

Most of the ingredients used in this book can be found in the supermarket, and this includes items such as coconut cream and vegetable stock cubes. Other ingredients may require a trip to a specialty food shop or delicatessen: grape leaves from a Greek grocery store, sun-dried tomatoes and olive paste from an Italian food shop, and tama-rind paste and garam masala from an Indian or Middle Eastern shop. Most of these specialty items are dried or bottled in oil or brine and do not take up much space on your shelves, so stock up with a few months' supply.

Vegetable stock

Vegetable stock cubes are easy to buy from all supermarkets, but mak-ing your own vegetable stock is just as easy. I save all my vegetable cooking water and boil it with a large onion, chopped (with skin on for color), carrots, celery, bay leaf, and parsley, and any other veg-etables that have begun to wither. The end result is strained and frozen in ice-cube trays for use in a recipe that calls for a particularly well-flavored stock.

Dried beans

As I mentioned earlier, canned beans are used throughout this book for convenience. If you want to use the dried variety, you will have to plan ahead. Most require overnight soaking in plenty of cold water to make them swell. Avoid quick soaking methods using boiling water; although the beans do seem to swell, they cause much more flatulence than those soaked overnight. I would also advise throwing away all soaking water or can water.

After overnight soaking, drain and cook beans in fresh water. Do not add any salt at this stage as it toughens the beans. Cook in boil-ing water until tender. Red kidney beans must be boiled hard for at least 10 minutes at the start of the cooking time to get rid of the toxin they contain.

Cooking times for different beans are given below but can only be an approximation, as cooking times will depend on how old a bean is, how long it has been soaked, and how hard the water is.

	Soaking time	Cooking time
Red kidney beans	overnight	10 minutes hard boiling plus 1 hour
Black-eyed peas	overnight	30-45 minutes
Navy beans	overnight	1 hour
Chickpeas	overnight	1 1/4 hours
Great Northern beans	overnight	1 1/4 hours
Cannellini beans	overnight	1 1/4 hours
Butterbeans	overnight	1 1/2 hours
Soybeans	at least 15 hours	2 hours

To peel tomatoes

Plunge whole tomatoes in boiling water, then remove immediately. The skins will peel off easily.

To toast nuts and seeds

Toasting brings out the flavor of nuts and seeds. The best way is to dry-fry them in a hot frying pan until lightly browned. Keep them moving in the hot pan or they will burn.

Serving quantities

All recipes throughout the book serve four unless otherwise stated.

MENU PLANNING

The traditional pattern for breakfast, lunch, and dinner probably fulfills the nutritional requirements as well as any, though there is some disagreement about the relative weight of the various meals. Some experts would have you eat like a king at breakfast, a prince at midday, and a pauper in the evening. Others suggest a light breakfast and supper with the main meal at midday. However, neither of these is a very convenient pattern today, and the family lifestyle is dictated as much by the kids' leisure activities as by habit.

In the past the main meal of the day consisted of three courses with a central main course, usually made up of a protein with vegetables. This pattern is changing now and there is no reason why the vegetarian should not choose two or three dishes of equal weight to serve as the main course. This might be preceded by a soup and/or simply followed with fruit. Following are some ideas for the main meal of the day, using recipes in this book. Finish with fruit, yogurt, or cheese.

Egg and Celery Soup ★ Mushroom and Walnut Risotto with Green Salad	Eggplant Pizza Slice ★ Cauliflower Soufflé Celery with Provence Herbs Baked Potatoes
Zuppa di Ceci ★ Cabbage Lorraine Leeks with Cashew Nuts Baked Potatoes	Roquefort and Celery Soup ★ Millet and Lentil Pilau Roman-Style Spinach Beets with Dill
Salade Ventoux ★ Pasta Ribbons with Spring Vegetables Tossed Salad	Stuffed Field Mushrooms ★ Greek Cheese Squares with Olives on Ciabatta Bread
Cauliflower and Grilled Red Pepper Salad ★ Bean and Cabbage Soup with Whole-Wheat Rolls	Bitter Salad with Grilled Red Peppers ★ Malaysian Vegetable-Fruit Curry Spiced Potatoes or Yams
Gazpacho ★ Zucchini with Pine Nuts and Orange Fava Beans in Tahini Sauce Fried Noodles with Watercress	Cabbage and Onion Casserole ★ Baked Sweet Potatoes Lettuce with Scallions and Peas Marinated Brie with Whole-Wheat Rolls

Soups, Starters, and Snacks

—◆—

SOUPS

—◆—

Home-made soups taste much better than the canned or packaged variety. There are only a few, such as Polish Egg and Dill Soup and Miso Soup, that need to be made at the last minute.

I try to make a double quantity of any recipe, and thus usually have a choice of two or three soups in store. Freeze in single or double portions for the most flexibility. The Egg and Celery Soup should be frozen without the eggs and tomato, but the rest will freeze well.

Soups like Bean and Cabbage Soup, Polish Egg and Dill Soup, Zuppa di Ceci, Vegetable Gumbo, and Lentil and Watercress Soup make filling main-course dishes served with plenty of whole-wheat bread or with a dollop of brown rice.

Curried Parsnip Soup

—◆—

Almost any root vegetable except perhaps beets can be substituted for parsnips in this recipe. The light curry flavor adds an extra dimension.

1 large onion, sliced
1 tablespoon vegetable oil
1 lb parsnips (about 4), chopped
1 tablespoon curry powder

3 cups vegetable stock
  (see page x)
salt and freshly ground black pepper

1. In a saucepan, fry the onion in the oil until lightly browned. Add the parsnips and curry powder and continue frying for 2-3 minutes.

2. Add the stock, season with salt and pepper, and bring to a boil. Cover and simmer for 30 minutes or until the parsnips are tender.

3. Purée in a blender or food processor or rub through a sieve. Reheat before serving.

Roquefort and Celery Root Soup with Croutons

Celery root gives a distinctive but delicate flavor to this soup. If you cannot find it, celery can be used instead, but you will need to add a large potato to ensure a good texture.

1 tablespoon vegetable oil
1 tablespoon butter
2 onions, sliced
1 lb celery root, chopped
1 carrot, chopped
2 1/2 cups vegetable stock (see page x)
freshly ground black pepper
1/2 cup light cream

4 oz Roquefort cheese, crumbled

Croutons
2 tablespoons softened butter or vegetable oil (optional)
2 slices of white bread, crusts removed
1 small clove garlic, crushed (optional)

1. In a saucepan, heat the oil with the butter and fry the onions, celery root, and carrot for 3-4 minutes to bring out the flavors. Add the stock and pepper and bring to a boil. Cover and simmer for 30 minutes.

2. Purée in a blender or food processor or rub through a sieve.

3. Return to the saucepan and add the cream and cheese. Carefully reheat without boiling, stirring constantly, until the cheese melts.

4. To make the croutons, spread the butter, if using, over each side of the slices of bread. Cut into strips and fry on both sides until crisp. Dice and use to garnish the soup.

To make garlic croutons, mash crushed garlic with the butter before spreading it on the bread.

Egg and Celery Soup

——◆——

The flavor of this Italian soup is much stronger than you would expect given the simplicity of the ingredients. This is due to the sweetness of the vegetables and the flavor of the olive oil.

SERVES 6

2 large onions, coarsely chopped
1 head of celery, sliced
2 tablespoons extra-virgin olive oil
2 1/2 cups vegetable stock (see page x)
salt and freshly ground black pepper

3 tomatoes, peeled (see page xi)
and halved
3 hard-boiled eggs, quartered
4 tablespoons chopped fresh parsley

1. In a saucepan, fry the onions and celery in the oil for 2-3 minutes, or until slightly softened. Add the stock, season with salt and pepper, and bring to a boil. Cover and simmer for 30 minutes.

2. Add the tomatoes and eggs and return to a boil for 2 minutes.

3. Ladle into soup bowls, making sure that everyone has half a tomato and 2 pieces of egg. Sprinkle with the chopped parsley.

Pepper and Zucchini Soup

——◆——

I am a great zucchini lover. I like them stuffed with flavored rice or cracked wheat, baked with onions and tomato, or steamed with fresh dill. This recipe is a good way of using up large, overgrown zucchini.

4 medium zucchini
2 peppers (preferably 1 red
  and 1 green), seeded
2 tablespoons vegetable oil

1 small bunch chives, 2-3 scallions,
  or a peeled shallot
2 basil sprigs
salt and freshly ground black pepper
3 cups water

1. Chop the flesh of the zucchini and peppers.

2. Heat the oil in a saucepan and add the vegetables. Sauté over low
   heat for 5 minutes or so. Add the remaining ingredients and bring
   to a boil. Cover and simmer for 30 minutes.

3. Purée in a blender or food processor or rub through a sieve. Reheat
   and serve.

Brussel Sprouts and Chestnut Soup

——◆——

This traditional combination of Brussel sprouts and chestnuts makes a
subtle soup. If using canned chestnuts, make sure they are not sweetened.

1 onion, chopped
1 tablespoon vegetable oil
1/4 cup dry sherry
1 lb Brussel sprouts, sliced
1/2 cup chestnuts, sliced, or 1/2 cup
  drained canned chestnuts

1 cup milk
2 cups vegetable stock (see page x)
salt and freshly ground black pepper
4 tablespoons light cream

1. In a saucepan, fry the onion in the oil until it turns translucent. Add
   the sherry and bring to a boil.

2. Add the remaining ingredients except the cream and return to a boil.
   Simmer for 20 minutes until the vegetables and chestnuts are tender.

3. Purée in a blender or food processor or rub through a sieve. Reheat
   and serve with a swirl of cream in each dish.

Tomato, Cauliflower, and Tarragon Soup

—◆—

The butter and sherry in this delightful soup are essential to the flavor, but olive oil and dry white wine can be used instead. The flavor will be different, but it will still taste good.

2 tablespoons butter
1 onion, chopped
1/4 cup dry sherry
2 cups chopped cauliflower
2 1/2 cups vegetable stock (see page x)

2-3 tablespoons chopped fresh tarra-
gon, or 1 teaspoon dried tarragon
1/2 teaspoon sugar
salt and freshly ground pepper

1. Melt the butter in a saucepan and fry the onion until lightly browned.

2. Add the sherry and bring to a boil. Add the remaining ingredients and simmer for 35 minutes.

3. Purée in a blender or food processor or rub through a sieve. Correct seasoning, if necessary, and serve sprinkled with a little more fresh tarragon.

Jerusalem Artichoke Soup

—◆—

Try this interesting Dutch soup with garlic croutons (see page 3). The recipe comes from some friends in The Hague who say that the garlic helps to bring out the flavor of the artichokes.

1 small onion, chopped
1 tablespoon vegetable oil
3/4 lb Jerusalem artichokes, washed
2 carrots, chopped

2 tomatoes, chopped
2 cups vegetable stock (see page x)
salt and freshly ground black pepper

1. In a saucepan, fry the onion in the oil until it turns translucent.

2. Meanwhile, peel the artichokes, wash again, chop, and add them to the pan. Work as quickly as possible, as they turn black rapidly.

3. Add the remaining ingredients. Bring to a boil, cover, and simmer for 30 minutes.

4. Purée in a blender or food processor or rub through a sieve. Reheat and serve.

Apple and Celery Soup

—◆—

This fruit-based soup actually comes from Germany, but it is typical of many countries in eastern Europe.

SERVES 12

2 tablespoons butter
3 onions, chopped
1/2 cup dry sherry or white vermouth
1 1/2 lbs apples, cored and chopped
1 head of celery, chopped

8 cups water
2 teaspoons ground cumin
salt and freshly ground black pepper
1/2 cup sour cream

1. Melt the butter in a saucepan and fry the onions until softened. Add the sherry or vermouth and bring to a boil.

2. Add the apple, celery, and water. Sprinkle with cumin, season with salt and pepper, and bring to a boil.

3. Purée in a blender or food processor. Add sour cream. Reheat before serving.

Lentil and Watercress Soup

——◆——

This is a lovely warming soup, ideal for winter weather. If you are in a hurry, omit the whole green lentils—the flavor will be just as good but the texture will not be as interesting.

SERVES 12

1 medium onion, sliced
1 tablespoon olive oil
1 lb carrots, chopped
1/2 cup red split lentils
3 large vegetable stock cubes
4 cups boiling water
2 parsley sprigs

1 fresh thyme sprig or
  1/4 teaspoon dried thyme
1 bay leaf
salt and freshly ground black pepper
1 bunch watercress
1/4 cup whole green lentils

1. In a saucepan, fry the onion in the oil until lightly browned. Add the carrots and cook over a very low heat for 3-4 minutes, stirring constantly. Add the split lentils, stock cubes, water, parsley, thyme, and bay leaf. Season with salt and pepper and bring to a boil. Reduce the heat and simmer for 30 minutes.

2. Remove the thyme and bay leaf. Add the watercress and cook for 5 more minutes. Purée in a blender or food processor or rub through a sieve.

3. Return to the heat and add the whole lentils. Simmer for 30 more minutes until the whole lentils are just cooked.

Vegetable Gumbo

—◆—

This filling soup from Louisiana can be made with different ingredients, but it should always contain okra and tabasco sauce. Go easy on the latter, or the soup will be very hot indeed!

1 large onion, chopped
1 garlic clove, crushed (optional)
2 peppers (1 red and 1 green),
  seeded and chopped
2 tablespoons vegetable oil
1 8-oz can of tomatoes
3/4 cup baby corn

4-5 celery stalks
2 cups vegetable stock (see page x)
salt and freshly ground pepper
dash of tabasco sauce, or to taste
1/2 cup long-grain rice
1/2 lb okra, washed and trimmed

1. In a saucepan, fry the onion, garlic, if using, and peppers in the oil for 3-4 minutes. Add the contents of the can of tomatoes and the remaining ingredients except the rice and okra. Bring to a boil and simmer for 20 minutes.

2. Meanwhile, put the rice in a separate saucepan with double its volume of salted boiling water. Cover and simmer for 13-14 minutes until all the liquid has been absorbed and the rice is tender.

3. Add the okra to the simmered vegetables and cook gently for 10 more minutes (gentle simmering is required to prevent the okra from splitting).

4. To serve, place small mounds of rice in each soup bowl and carefully spoon the soup.

Zuppa di Ceci

— ◆ —

This chickpea soup is typical of Lombardy, Italy. In other areas carrots and celery are included, but I feel they are unnecessary because of the wonderful flavor of the mushrooms. If fresh sage is not available, use 1/4 teaspoon dried sage instead, and add it with the salt and pepper.

1/2 oz dried Italian mushrooms or cèpes
1 large onion, coarsely chopped
2 garlic cloves, crushed
2 tablespoons olive oil
1 14-oz can of chickpeas, drained
1 tablespoon flour

2 1/2 cups vegetable stock (see page x)
1 teaspoon tomato purée
salt and freshly ground black pepper
6-8 romaine lettuce leaves, shredded
1 sage sprig
extra-virgin olive oil, to taste

1. Soak the mushrooms in a saucepan in just enough boiling water to cover them.

2. In a separate saucepan, fry the onion and garlic in the oil until lightly browned.

3. Toss the chickpeas in flour and add to the saucepan containing the mushrooms and their soaking water. Add the stock, tomato purée, salt, and pepper. Bring to a boil and simmer for 15-20 minutes.

4. Add the lettuce and sage and simmer for 1 more minute. Serve at once with a little extra-virgin olive oil poured into the soup.

Hungarian Apple Soup

— ◆ —

I first encountered this unusual, slightly sweet soup on a visit to Lake Balaton in Hungary. A specialty in a lakeside restaurant, it was served with large chunks of rye bread.

2 onions, chopped
1 garlic clove, chopped
4 apples, cored and diced
1 red pepper, seeded and chopped
1 large pickled cucumber, diced
2 tablespoons vegetable oil

2 1/2 cups vegetable stock
  (see page x)
1/2 teaspoon paprika
2 tablespoons chopped chives
1/2 cup sour cream
1 cup fresh breadcrumbs (optional)

1. In a saucepan, fry the onions, garlic, apples, pepper, and pickled cucumber in the oil. After 3-4 minutes add the stock and paprika. Bring to a boil and simmer for 20 minutes.

2. Remove from the heat and stir in half the chives and the sour cream. Serve sprinkled with the remaining chives.

3. For a slightly thicker soup, stir in the breadcrumbs.

Miso Soup

——◆——

This traditional Japanese soup uses seaweed, tofu, and miso. Dried seaweed and miso, a fermented bean paste, can be found in most health food stores. It is important not to overcook miso, so add it just before serving. Do not allow the soup to boil after you have added it.

1 oz dried Japanese seaweed (kombu)
2 1/2 cups vegetable stock
  (see page x)

1 tablespoon miso
1/4 lb tofu, sliced
6 scallions, trimmed and sliced

1. Reconstitute the seaweed as directed on the package.

2. Heat the stock in a saucepan and add the seaweed and its soaking water. Bring to a boil and cook the seaweed according to the package directions.

3. Remove from the heat and stir in the miso.

4. Divide the tofu and scallions among 4 soup bowls and pour in the soup. Serve at once.

Bean and Cabbage Soup

—◆—

This soup is based on an Italian recipe called Riollita, which is made with cabbage and beans. In Italy it is cooked until it is quite thick and then served on large hunks of bread.

SERVES 4-6 as a main course

1 medium onion, finely chopped
1 garlic clove, finely chopped
1 small fresh rosemary sprig
1 bay leaf
1 tablespoon olive oil
2 celery stalks, thinly sliced
1 carrot, finely diced

1 tablespoon tomato purée
6 cups vegetable stock (see page x)
1 14-oz can of cannellini or
   Great Northern beans, drained
1/2 small to medium Savoy cabbage,
   shredded
salt and freshly ground black pepper

1. In a saucepan, fry the onion, garlic, rosemary, and bay leaf in the oil for 3-4 minutes. Add the celery and carrot and continue cooking for 5 more minutes to soften but not brown.

2. Remove the herbs and add the tomato purée and stock. Bring to a boil and simmer for 15 minutes.

3. Rub half of the beans through a sieve and add them to the soup. Add the remaining beans (whole) and the cabbage. Season with salt and pepper, if desired, and simmer for 10 more minutes.

Iced Cucumber Soup

—◆—

The delicate flavor of this soup is best appreciated when it is chilled.

2 tablespoons butter or
  1 1/2 tablespoons vegetable oil
1 medium onion, sliced
1/2 cup dry white wine
1/2 lb potatoes, peeled and sliced
1/2 large cucumber, chopped
2 cups vegetable stock (see page x)

salt and freshly ground black pepper

Garnishes
4 tablespoons yogurt or light
  cream
1 cucumber, diced
parsley or chervil sprigs

1. Heat the butter or oil in a saucepan and fry the onion until lightly browned. Add the wine and bring to a boil. Add the potatoes, cucumber, and stock. Season with salt and pepper. Simmer for 30 minutes, then allow to cool.

2. Blend and correct seasoning, if necessary. Let the soup cool, then refrigerate it. To serve, garnish with a swirl of yogurt or cream, cucumber, and parsley or chervil sprigs.

Chilled Beet Soup

—◆—

The sour cream gives this soup a pretty marbled effect.

2 tablespoons butter or firm
  margarine
1 medium onion, finely chopped
1 garlic clove, crushed

3 medium beets, cooked and chopped
2 cups vegetable stock (see page x)
salt and freshly ground black pepper
1/2 cup sour cream

1. Melt the butter or margarine in a saucepan and fry the onion and garlic until softened but not browned. Add the beets and stock. Season with salt and pepper and bring to a boil.

2. Blend until smooth and allow to cool. Chill for at least 4 hours. Before serving, stir in the sour cream.

Chilled Fennel Soup

—◆—

Although we associate fennel mainly with Italy, this unusual soup is actually based on a British recipe that was popular as long ago as the fourteenth century. You may be surprised to discover that it is thickened with ground almonds.

1 large or 2 smaller heads
  of fresh fennel
1 1/2 cups water
1/2 cup dry white wine

salt and freshly ground black pepper
1 oz ground almonds
2/3 cup yogurt

1. Trim the fennel, retaining a little of the feathery green tops for garnish. Coarsely chop the fennel root and the rest of the tops. Place in a saucepan with the water and wine. Season with salt and pepper. Bring to a boil, cover, and simmer for 30 minutes.

2. Purée in a blender or food processor or rub through a sieve. Return to the saucepan and stir in the ground almonds. Bring back to a boil and simmer 15 more minutes, stirring occasionally. Remove from the heat and let cool.

3. Blend in the yogurt and chill for at least 30 minutes before serving. Garnish with the finely chopped fennel leaves.

Polish Egg and Dill Soup

—◆—

This soup has a lovely texture with the smooth yogurt contrasting with the crunchy vegetables. It's quick to prepare, and you can add almost any flavorings. Try tomato and basil in place of the eggs and dill. Serve as a main course with crusty Whole-Wheat Rolls (see page 128).

1 cup thinly sliced cucumber
2 carrots, grated or finely shredded
4 tablespoons chopped fresh dill
2 1/2 cups low-fat yogurt
4 hard-boiled eggs, roughly chopped

12-16 fresh spinach leaves,
  finely shredded
salt and freshly ground black pepper
dill sprigs

1. Cut the cucumber slices in half and retain a few for garnish along with some grated or shredded carrot.

2. Place the remaining ingredients in a large bowl and mix well. Chill for half an hour.

3. Serve in individual bowls garnished with cucumber, carrots, and dill.

Gazpacho

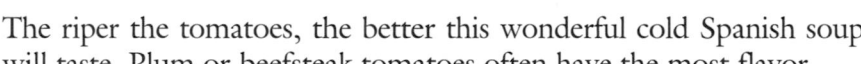

The riper the tomatoes, the better this wonderful cold Spanish soup will taste. Plum or beefsteak tomatoes often have the most flavor.

2 lbs very ripe tomatoes, peeled
  (see page xi), seeded, and chopped
1 red pepper, seeded and chopped
3/4 cup diced cucumber
2 tablespoons finely chopped scallions
1 teaspoon chopped garlic
5 tablespoons cider or wine vinegar
4 tablespoons extra-virgin olive oil

1 1/2 tablespoons tomato purée
3/4-1 cup water

Garnishes
1/2 red pepper, seeded and diced
1/2 green pepper, seeded and diced
1 cucumber, diced

1. Place the tomato, pepper, cucumber, scallions, and garlic in a blender or food processor with the vinegar. Blend until smooth.

2. Stir in the remaining ingredients and chill for 1 hour.

3. Prepare the garnishes just before serving and place in separate bowls for guests to sprinkle onto their soup.

STARTERS

——◆——

The recipes in this section make a good start to a meal, but many of them can be adapted to serve as snacks or light main-course dishes. Try Mushroom and Fennel Salad or Shropska in pita bread, for example. Or add some mozzarella cheese to the Grapefruit and Avocado Salad or the Three-Fruit Salad. You can also increase the quantity of cottage cheese in the Avocado and Orange Platter.

Mushrooms and Chickpeas à la Grecque can be served hot with baked potatoes, and Salade Ventoux goes well with other salads. Japanese Fried Tofu, Eggplant Pizza Slices, Two Mushroom Combo, and Mediterranean Eggplant can all be increased in quantity to make more substantial dishes.

Mushroom and Fennel Salad

——◆——

The flavors of these two vegetables complement each other particularly well. Serve as a starter on a bed of lettuce or create a more elaborate dish by adding melon balls.

*2 small heads or 1 large head
    of fresh fennel
salt and freshly ground black pepper
1/2 lb button mushrooms,
    quartered or chopped*

*4 tablespoons mayonnaise
pinch of dried thyme or mixed herbs
1 small honeydew melon, seeded
    and scooped into balls (optional)
salad leaves*

1. Trim the fennel and blanch in a little boiling salted water for 3-4 minutes, or steam for 5-6 minutes in a steamer. Drain, cool, and chop.

2. Mix with the remaining ingredients, including the melon balls, if desired. Serve on a bed of salad leaves.

16

Grapefruit and Avocado Salad

—◆—

Fried breadcrumbs add texture to this simple and refreshing salad. Pink grapefruit is usually sweeter than the ordinary yellow grapefruit, so choose which type according to how astringent you like your first course.

1 slice of whole-wheat bread
1 bunch parsley
salt and freshly ground black pepper
2 tablespoons olive oil
2 grapefruit, peeled and segmented
  (reserve the juice)
2 avocados, halved

oregano, basil, and Italian parsley
  small sprigs

Dressing
3 tablespoons extra-virgin olive oil
2 teaspoons red wine vinegar
salt and freshly ground black pepper

1. Chop the bread and parsley in a blender or food processor. Mix with plenty of salt and pepper. Heat the oil in a frying pan and add the breadcrumb mixture. Fry slowly until well browned all over, stirring constantly.

2. Arrange the grapefruit segments in the center of 4 serving plates. Slice the avocado and place the slices between the grapefruit segments. Sprinkle with the breadcrumb mixture. Roughly chop the herbs and sprinkle on top.

3. Mix the reserved grapefruit juice with the oil and vinegar and season with salt and pepper. Pour the dressing over the salads. Serve at once.

Artichokes with Dressing

——◆——

This is my favorite dressing for large artichokes. Its fresh and piquant flavor matches that of the artichoke. Knock off the stems before cooking the artichokes by hitting them with a rolling pin or hammer. This way, the stems will come off with long stringy bits attached to them, whereas if you cut them off with a knife, these bits remain in the heart of the artichoke.

4 large artichokes, stems removed (see above)
1 lemon, sliced
1/2 lb cottage cheese or other low-fat soft cheese
2 tablespoons milk or water

1 tablespoon red wine vinegar
4-5 radishes, finely chopped
3-4 pickled cucumbers, finely chopped
1 tablespoon chopped fresh basil
salt and freshly ground black pepper

1. Boil the artichokes in a large pan of water with the sliced lemon. This will help them retain their color. Cook for about 45 minutes until they are very soft in the base. Drain and let cool, then remove and discard the center leaves and the hairy part of the artichoke.

2. Blend the cheese, milk or water, and vinegar to a smooth cream. Stir in the remaining ingredients and serve with the cold artichokes.

Marinated Zucchini

—◆—

This dish from Provence can be kept in the refrigerator for a day or two, as it improves each day. The flavor depends very much on the use of sage, although this is not typical of the region.

2 large zucchini
4 tablespoons olive oil, divided
salt and freshly ground black pepper
1 garlic clove, chopped

1 tablespoon chopped fresh sage
  or 1 teaspoon dried sage
1 tablespoon red wine vinegar
1/2 cup dry white wine

1. Trim the zucchini and cut it into thick diagonal slices. Fry the pieces in a frying pan in 2 tablespoons of the oil until lightly browned on each side. Pack them into a pâté dish, seasoning each layer with salt and pepper.

2. Pour the remaining oil into the pan and fry the garlic and sage until the garlic is brown. Add the vinegar and wine and bring to a boil.

3. Pour the hot liquid over the zucchini so that they are fully covered. Cover with foil, let cool, and chill for at least an hour before serving.

Avocado and Orange Platter

—◆—

Avocado mixes well with all citrus fruit, and although this recipe uses oranges, you could just as easily use grapefruit. Make just before serving or the avocados will discolor.

2 large oranges, peeled and sliced
  into rounds
2 large avocados, sliced into lengths

4 tablespoons low-fat soft cheese
1 tablespoon chopped cashew nuts
1 tablespoon chopped raisins

1. Arrange the orange rounds on 4 individual plates and place 2 or 3 slices of avocado between them.

2. Mix the remaining ingredients together and place a spoonful in the center of each plate. Serve at once.

Vinaigrette Vegetables

—◆—

Wherever you go on the Mediterranean coast—Italy, Spain, and France—you will find a version of this recipe. All kinds of vegetables can be cooked, coated with a well-flavored vinaigrette while still warm, then chilled. There is no reason why you should not mix and match the vegetables and dressings to suit your own particular tastes, though I can strongly recommend the Honey Vinaigrette on fennel, and the Walnut and Tarragon Vinaigrette on zucchini.

Vegetables to choose from

1 lb zucchini, steamed and sliced or
    steamed whole baby leeks or
    steamed and sliced fennel root or
    steamed and sliced grilled eggplant or
    seeded and grilled red peppers

Dressings

1. French Vinaigrette

6 tablespoons olive oil
1 1/2 tablespoons red wine vinegar
salt and freshly ground black pepper
a little mustard (optional)

2. Walnut and Tarragon Vinaigrette

6 tablespoons walnut oil
2 tablespoons tarragon vinegar
1 teaspoon freshly chopped shallots or scallions
salt and freshly ground black pepper

3. Honey Vinaigrette

6 tablespoons olive oil
1 tablespoon cider vinegar
2 teaspoons honey
1 teaspoon grainy mustard
salt and freshly ground black pepper

Guacamole-Stuffed Tomatoes

—◆—

Use the recipe on page 161 to make this smooth Mexican avocado dip, and use it as the Spanish do, to stuff tomatoes.

1/2 quantity guacamole   *salt and freshly ground black pepper*
(see page 161)   *fresh cilantro sprigs*
4 large tomatoes

1. Prepare the guacamole and cover with plastic wrap. Set aside.

2. Slice the tops off the tomatoes and discard. Dig out the center seeds with a teaspoon and discard.

3. Season the inside of the tomatoes with salt and pepper and spoon in the guacamole. Garnish with sprigs of cilantro.

Shropska

—◆—

The fresh, clean taste of this crunchy Bulgarian salad makes it a very good summer dish. I usually serve it as a first course, but it could also be served as a side salad.

4 large tomatoes   *salt and freshly ground black pepper*
1 small onion   *4 oz cheddar cheese, grated*
1/2 green pepper, seeded   *(about 1 cup)*
1 small cucumber   *juice of 1 lemon*
3-4 celery stalks

1. Coarsely chop the vegetables and layer in individual bowls. Season with salt and pepper and top with cheese and lemon juice.

2. Chill for half an hour before serving.

Three-Fruit Salad

——◆——

One tends to think of fruit salad as a dessert, but this mixture makes a very good first course or lunch snack. Buy the best balsamic vinegar you can afford, as some of the cheaper ones don't have the characteristic full fruity flavor.

2 kiwi fruit, peeled and sliced
1 large pink or red grapefruit,
* peeled and segmented*
2 tomatoes, sliced
mixed salad leaves
2 tablespoons pine nuts, toasted
* (see page xi)*

1 tablespoon small black olives
fresh parsley sprigs

Dressing
5 tablespoons extra-virgin olive oil
1/2 teaspoon balsamic vinegar
salt and freshly ground black pepper

1. Arrange the kiwi, grapefruit, and tomatoes in an overlapping rosette on 4 plates. Place a few salad leaves around the outside. Strew the pine nuts and olives lightly over the plates and dot with parsley.

2. Mix the dressing ingredients together and sprinkle on the fruit.

Chickpeas à la Grecque

——◆——

I stumbled on this excellent variation of Mushrooms à la Grecque when I was thinking of ideas for using up some canned chickpeas. They give an interesting texture to this traditional dish, but you could of course revert to the original by leaving the chickpeas out and adding more button mushrooms.

2 small onions, sliced
4 tablespoons olive oil
1/2 pound button mushrooms
1/2 cup canned chickpeas, drained
2 cups dry white wine

2 teaspoons tomato purée
1/2 teaspoon dried oregano
1 bay leaf
1/4 teaspoon fennel or coriander seeds
salt and freshly ground black pepper

1. In a saucepan, fry the onions in 2 tablespoons of the oil until transparent. Add the mushrooms, halved if necessary, and chickpeas. Pour in the wine and add the remaining ingredients. Bring to a boil and simmer for 30 minutes.

2. Serve chilled.

Salade Ventoux

—◆—

I came across this dish on a visit to the Provence olive oil harvest one December. The sun was shining but it was quite cold, and this warm salad made a great lunchtime starter.

4 small green peppers, quartered and seeded
1/2 lb soft goat cheese
8 tablespoons extra-virgin olive oil

3 tablespoons raisins, plumped in warm water
2 tablespoons pine nuts, toasted (see page xi)
1 teaspoon balsamic vinegar

1. Place the peppers skin side up under a hot broiler and cook until well charred. Transfer them to a soup bowl and cover with a plate. Let them stand for half an hour and then peel.

2. Cut the cheese into 4 thick slices and place in a warm, not hot, oven.

3. Heat the oil in a pan with the raisins until they just begin to sizzle. Add the pine nuts and vinegar and remove from the heat.

4. Arrange the peppers on 4 warm plates. Add the cheese and spoon the olive oil mixture over the top. Serve at once.

Fried Kale with Almonds

—◆—

Treated in this way, curly kale tastes exactly like deep-fried seaweed served in some Chinese restaurants—not surprising really, since it is in fact cabbage and not seaweed that they use. Serve this dish as a starter to a Chinese-style meal or as an accompaniment with other vegetables.

1 small bunch curly kale
2 tablespoons sliced almonds

vegetable oil for frying

1. Remove the stalks from the kale and shred the leaves very finely. Mix with the almonds.

2. Pour about 1/2 inch of vegetable oil into a large heavy-bottomed pan. Heat until very hot. Drop half the kale mixture into the pan and stir.

3. When all the kale is crispy (this happens very quickly), remove it with a slotted spoon and drain on paper towels. Repeat the process with the remaining kale mixture. Drain and serve at once.

Love Apples

—◆—

It took me three tries before I managed to reproduce this delicious special-occasion starter which I first tasted in a restaurant in the Conway Valley in North Wales. The cheese and cream should not be added too soon, because you want the end result to be runny rather than set.

8 tomatoes, peeled (see page xi)
and sliced
1 cup (approximately) dry or
medium-dry sherry

salt and freshly ground black pepper
1 oz cheddar cheese, grated
(about 1 cup)
1/4 cup whipping cream

1. Preheat the oven to 350°F.

2. Divide the tomatoes among 4 small ramekin dishes. Pour in enough sherry to cover, and season with salt and pepper. Bake in the oven for 20 minutes.

3. Sprinkle each dish with cheese and cream and continue cooking 4-5 more minutes. Serve at once.

Japanese Fried Tofu

—◆—

This is a classic Japanese way of serving tofu. It is often served on its own as an additional course between soup and the main dish.

1/2 lb tofu
1 tablespoon vegetable oil
2 tablespoons light soy sauce
or 1 tablespoon soy sauce
2 tablespoons rice vinegar
or medium sherry

1 teaspoon grated fresh ginger
1/2 cup water
1 teaspoon miso
2 scallions, finely chopped

1. Cut the tofu into 4 rectangular pieces. Heat the oil in a nonstick frying pan and fry the tofu on all sides to seal. Place in small individual bowls.

2. Heat the soy sauce, vinegar or sherry, ginger, and water in a saucepan. Just before the mixture boils, remove from the heat and stir in the miso.

3. Pour this mixture over the tofu. Let cool to lukewarm. Sprinkle with scallions and serve.

Eggplant Pizza Slices

—◆—

Since this is one of my favorite first courses, I make double and triple quantities of the tomato sauce and freeze it. I prefer to use Pecorino cheese as it has a strong, piquant flavor. Mozzarella has a lighter, slightly stringy effect.

4 ripe tomatoes, peeled (see page xi) and sliced, plus 1/2 cup tomato juice or 1 14-oz can of tomatoes
1 teaspoon tomato purée
1 garlic clove, crushed

fresh or dried thyme leaves
salt and freshly ground black pepper
2 long, thin eggplants
olive oil
4 oz Pecorino or mozzarella cheese, sliced

1. In a saucepan, mix the tomatoes and juice (or the contents of the can of tomatoes) with the tomato purée and garlic, and boil until fairly thick. Leave to cool, then season with the thyme and salt and pepper.

2. Cut each eggplant into 16 slices, about 1/2 inch thick. Brush the slices with oil and place under the broiler. Broil 8-10 minutes, turning occasionally.

3. Spread the tomato sauce on the broiled eggplant and cover with slices of cheese. Return to the broiler and cook for 2-3 minutes, or until the cheese bubbles.

Garlic Mushrooms

—◆—

Choose mushrooms with open caps for easier stuffing.

1 lb mushrooms, wiped clean
vegetable oil
4 tablespoons butter, softened
2 garlic cloves, crushed
2 tablespoons chopped fresh parsley

pinch of dried thyme
salt and freshly ground black pepper
2 teaspoons lemon juice
2 oz fresh breadcrumbs (about 1 1/2 cups)

1. In a frying pan, fry the mushrooms in hot oil for about 20 seconds, then drain them on paper towels. Place them in a shallow baking pan, stem side up.

2. In a bowl, mix together the butter, garlic, parsley, thyme, salt, pepper, and lemon juice. Spoon some of the mixture into each mushroom, then lightly press the breadcrumbs on top.

3. Cook under the broiler for 5 minutes, or until the breadcrumbs are golden brown.

Two Mushroom Combo

There is an Eastern feel to this recipe, which uses mushrooms to stuff mushrooms. If you do not have a microwave oven, bake these in a conventional oven for about 15-20 minutes at 400°F. The secret of this dish lies in careful cooking. Do not overcook the mushrooms or they will shrink too much.

4 medium portobello mushrooms
5 tablespoons olive oil, divided
1 large garlic clove, crushed
salt and freshly ground black pepper
6 oz oyster mushrooms, sliced

1 tablespoon soy sauce
3 tablespoons dry white wine
sliced rind of 2 kumquats
pinch of five-spice powder
1 bunch fresh chives

1. Place the portobellos in a large shallow dish. In a bowl, mix 4 tablespoons of the oil with the garlic, salt, and pepper, and pour it over the mushrooms. Cook in a microwave for 3-4 minutes depending on the mushroom size (or see oven instructions above). The juices should be running but the mushrooms should still retain some of their bite.

2. Heat the remaining oil in a skillet and sauté the sliced oyster mushrooms for 1 minute. Add the soy sauce, wine, kumquat rind, and five-spice powder. Bring to a boil and boil rapidly for a couple of minutes.

3. Arrange sprigs of chives on each plate, place the portabellos in the center, and top with the oyster mushrooms and juices.

Mediterranean Eggplant

—◆—

The flavor in this dish depends on the typical Mediterranean ingredients of olive oil, olives, and capers. This unusual stuffing can also be used on grilled radicchio.

2 small to medium eggplants,
halved lengthwise
12 black olives, pitted and chopped
4 tablespoons pine nuts,
very lightly toasted (see page xi)
4 tablespoons chopped fresh parsley

2 tablespoons raisins
2 garlic cloves, finely chopped
1 oregano sprig
2 tomatoes, very thinly sliced
olive oil

1. Preheat the oven to 450°F.

2. Place the eggplant halves in a baking dish cut side up, and slash with a criss-cross pattern.

3. In a bowl, mix the remaining ingredients together except for the tomatoes and oil.

4. Spread the mixture over the top of the eggplant halves. Cover with tomato slices and drizzle with oil. Bake for at least an hour.

SNACKS

——◆——

These are my favorite snack foods. Some take quite a while to prepare, but can be made the day or even the week before and stored in the refrigerator or freezer.

Hummus, Falafel, and Italian Crunchy Cheese Balls freeze well. They are good served on their own, with salad, or in pita bread. Spring Rolls and Vegetable Samosas also freeze well.

Some of the recipes in the buffet food chapter such as Pâtés de Béziers, Onion and Black Olive Tart, Celery Root and Carrot Flan, and Savory Pumpkin Plait also make good snacks and freeze well in single portions. They are particularly useful for packed lunches since single portions usually thaw by lunchtime, although I try to remember to take them out of the freezer the night before.

Eggs with Broccoli

——◆——

This is a very quick way of brightening up scrambled eggs. The soy sauce adds tang to the broccoli.

1 1/2 lbs broccoli florets   *salt and freshly ground black pepper*
6-8 eggs, beaten   *2 tablespoons tamari or soy sauce*
4 tablespoons water

1. Steam the broccoli until just tender. Break up florets.

2. In a bowl, mix the eggs with water and season with salt and pepper. Scramble the eggs in the usual way, then place them in the center of 4 warm plates.

3. Toss the broccoli in the tamari or soy sauce and spoon it around the outside of the egg.

Pipérade

—◆—

This scrambled egg dish with garlic, peppers, and tomatoes comes from the Basque area of southern France. Spain has a similar dish, but the eggs are set rather than scrambled.

4 red peppers, seeded and quartered
3 tablespoons olive oil
1 onion, sliced
1 garlic clove, sliced
4 tomatoes, peeled (see page xi)
*   and cut into chunks*

1/2 green chile pepper, seeded and
*   chopped*
1 bay leaf
fresh thyme sprig
6 eggs
2 tablespoons water
salt and freshly ground black pepper

1. Broil the peppers until the skins blister. Place them in a soup bowl and cover with a plate. Let them stand, then peel and cut them into strips.

2. Heat the oil in a heavy pan and fry the onion and garlic until softened. Add the peppers, tomatoes, chile, bay leaf, and thyme. Cook over low heat for 30 minutes, stirring occasionally.

3. Beat the eggs and water together and season with salt and pepper. Pour into a frying pan. When the eggs start to set, stir in the pepper mixture and continue cooking and stirring until the eggs are lightly scrambled.

Falafel with Tahini Sauce

——◆——

This Middle Eastern snack has become an Israeli specialty. It can be served in pita bread with lettuce, onions, and tomatoes.

1 14-oz can of chickpeas, drained
1/2 small onion, chopped
1 garlic clove, crushed
1 teaspoon ground cumin
1/2 teaspoon ground coriander
1/2 teaspoon baking powder
pinch of cayenne
1 tablespoon flour
4 tablespoons chopped fresh parsley
1 tablespoon chopped fresh cilantro

salt and freshly ground black pepper
1 egg yolk
water
vegetable oil for deep-frying

Tahini Sauce
4 tablespoons tahini paste
3 tablespoons lemon juice
pinch of salt
1 tablespoon cold water

1. Mince the chickpeas or grind them in a food processor. Place them in a bowl and mix in the onion, garlic, cumin, coriander, baking powder, and cayenne. Add the flour, parsley, cilantro, salt, and pepper. Bind with the egg yolk. (You may need a little water as well.)

2. Shape into walnut-sized balls and deep-fry them in oil. Drain on paper towels.

3. To make the sauce, mix the tahini and lemon juice in a blender or food processor. Add a little salt and only enough water to give a consistency a little thicker than light cream.

4. Serve the balls stuffed into pita bread with salad and a little sauce on top.

Italian Crunchy Cheese Balls

—◆—

You need to use Italian arborio rice for this recipe. Because it is stickier than long-grain rice, it helps to hold the balls together.

You can prepare the balls without the breadcrumbs ahead of time and refrigerate or freeze them, but allow more frying time if they're frozen. The balls are soft on the inside and crisp on the outside.

Serve them with salad or coleslaw, or eat them with your fingers.

MAKES 16

3/4 Italian arborio rice	*1 teaspoon dried oregano*
salt and freshly ground black pepper	*1 teaspoon tomato purée*
1 egg, beaten	*2 oz dried breadcrumbs*
6 oz flavorful cheese	*vegetable oil for deep-frying*

1. In a saucepan, cook the rice in salted water for 10-12 minutes until just tender. Drain well, and in a bowl mix with the remaining ingredients except the breadcrumbs and oil.

2. Place in the refrigerator for a couple of hours to chill.

3. Shape the mixture into balls, roll in breadcrumbs, and deep-fry for 2-3 minutes. Drain well on paper towels.

Indian Toast

—◆—

This is an Indian version of cheese on toast. For a more substantial snack, crown the spicy topping with a poached egg.

4 oz cheddar cheese, grated	*1 teaspoon curry powder*
(about 1 cup)	*4 large slices of bread*
2 tablespoons mango chutney	*4 tomatoes, sliced*

1. In a bowl, mix the cheese, chutney, and curry powder to a thick paste.

2. Toast the bread under the broiler on both sides. Cover with tomato slices and top with the cheese mixture.

3. Return to the broiler for 3-4 minutes, or until the cheese is bubbly.

Italian Bruschetta

———◆———

This Italian dish has become very popular beyond the shores of the Mediterranean. It was originally served as an appetizer, but makes a quick snack. Use *ciabatta* (flat Italian bread loaves) or fresh French bread.

1 large flat Italian bread loaf   *4-5 basil sprigs*
  or 2 short French loaves   *6 tomatoes, sliced*
2 garlic cloves   *salt and freshly ground black pepper*
6 tablespoons olive oil   *grated Parmesan cheese (optional)*

1. Slice the bread in half lengthwise. Rub the cut sides with the garlic cloves, leaving bits of garlic behind. Then brush with oil.

2. Bake in a 450°F oven for 8-10 minutes, or toast under the broiler for 4-5 minutes each side. Dot with basil and arrange slices of tomato over the top.

3. Season with salt and pepper and place under the broiler for 1-2 more minutes. Add Parmesan, if desired.

Popovers

—◆—

These whole-wheat puffs are quick to make, and are delicious served with maple syrup. Try them for breakfast.

4 eggs, separated　　　　　　　*5 tablespoons whole-wheat flour*
2 cups milk　　　　　　　　　*1 teaspoon salt*

1. Preheat the oven to 450°F. Grease a muffin pan with butter or oil.

2. In a bowl, beat the egg yolks until they are stiff and pale yellow in color. Add the milk and flour alternately, beating constantly.

3. Add the salt to the egg whites in another bowl and whisk until they are very stiff. Stir 1 tablespoon of the whites into the yolk mixture and then carefully fold in the rest.

4. Spoon into the greased muffin pan and bake for 30 minutes. Serve straight from the oven.

Hummus

—◆—

Serve as a dip as they do in Greek and Cypriot restaurants, in sandwiches, or as a snack or starter with pita bread and raw vegetables.

1 1-lb can of chickpeas, drained　　　*2-3 tablespoons olive oil*
2 tablespoons tahini paste
1-2 garlic cloves, crushed　　　　　**Garnishes**
juice of 1 lemon　　　　　　　　*ground cumin*
salt　　　　　　　　　　　　*paprika*
　　　　　　　　　　　　　　Italian parsley sprigs

1. Rub the chickpeas through a sieve or blend in a food processor. Add the remaining ingredients except the oil and blend well.

2. Spoon into a bowl, pour on the oil, and garnish with the cumin, paprika, and parsley.

Open Sandwiches

———◆———

Danish open sandwiches are much more attractive than traditional closed ones and are very quick to make. Use at least two major ingredients along with a garnish. Try to get some height into the topping by arranging the toppings over lettuce leaves or by heaping up small spoonfuls of chopped ingredients.

The Base

Any kind of firm, thick-cut bread can be used. The Danes prefer rye bread for its taste and density. Butter liberally—this is what keeps the topping in place.

Toppings

1. Chopped egg and onion (see page 164) on a bed of watercress with sliced tomatoes and capers.

2. Sliced cooked beets on lettuce with orange segments and horseradish sauce; garnish with parsley.

3. Cheddar cheese and carrot, both grated, piled over alfalfa or watercress with sliced cucumber and fresh tarragon.

4. Sliced avocado with cranberry jelly and cottage cheese.

5. Sliced blue cheese with halved grapes and sliced celery over lettuce.

6. Sliced mushrooms with walnut halves and shredded lettuce on mayonnaise instead of butter.

7. Hummus (see page 34) with black olives and sliced tomatoes on lettuce with freshly chopped mixed herbs.

8. Watercress with apple slices on peanut butter instead of butter.

Savory Muffins

——◆——

It's easy to rustle up these moist, flavorful muffins. Serve warm. If there are any left over, store in an airtight container and reheat before serving.

MAKES 16

1 1/4 cups whole-wheat flour
4 level teaspoons baking powder
1/2 teaspoon salt
2 large eggs
1 cup milk
4 tablespoons butter or margarine,
  melted
1/2 cup coarsely grated carrots
2 tablespoons sunflower seeds

Flavoring 1
4 tablespoons grated cheddar cheese

Flavoring 2
1/4 cup canned or frozen corn
  kernels with chopped green pepper
6 stuffed olives

1. Preheat the oven to 375°F. Grease a muffin pan with oil.

2. In a bowl, mix the flour, baking powder, and salt.

3. In another bowl, whisk the eggs with the milk and melted butter, and pour over the dry ingredients. Mix together and add the carrots, sunflower seeds, and a flavoring.

4. Spoon into the prepared muffin pan. Do not fill too full. Bake 45-50 minutes, or until springy to the touch. Let the muffins cool a little before serving.

Fried Feta Cheese with Capers

——◆——

A Greek restaurant near my home serves this tasty dish as a starter, but it could make a good snack with plenty of crusty bread.

4 thick slices of feta cheese
shredded iceberg lettuce
1/2 small onion, cut in rings
tomato and lemon wedges

6 tablespoons warm olive oil
4 tablespoons drained capers
fresh ground black pepper

1. Place the cheese under a broiler until lightly browned on both sides.

2. Arrange a small mound of lettuce topped with an onion ring on 4 plates.

3. Place a slice of the broiled cheese on top of each lettuce-onion mound. Arrange tomato and lemon wedges on the side. Pour the oil over and sprinkle with capers and black pepper.

Onion Bread

—◆—

This unusual bread comes from Syria. Try it warm with hard-boiled eggs, black olives, and salad.

MAKES 1 LOAF

1 small onion, finely chopped
3 tablespoons olive oil
1 cup self-rising flour
1/2 teaspoon salt

1 teaspoon baking powder
1/2 teaspoon dried thyme
milk

1. In a frying pan, fry the onion in the oil until transparent.

2. Sift the flour, salt, and baking powder into a bowl. Add the thyme and mix well with a spoon. Make a well in the center and add the fried onions and sufficient water to make a fairly soft dough.

3. Turn out onto a floured surface and knead for about 10 minutes until the dough is elastic and no longer sticks to your hands. Place in a 1-lb loaf pan and let it rest in a warm place for about 10 minutes.

4. Preheat the oven to 350°F.

5. Brush the top of the loaf with milk. Bake for about 1 hour and 20 minutes, or until golden on top and a skewer inserted into the center comes out clean. Remove from the pan and let it cool on a wire rack.

Baked Potatoes with Toppings

—◆—

Baked potatoes take about 1 hour in the oven at 400°F. Or, if you do not mind limp skins, they can be cooked very quickly in the microwave. A combination of both cooking methods works well.

The potato stuffing recipes given here are sufficient for 4 large baking potatoes.

1. Leeks with Caraway

4 tablespoons butter
1 1/2 lbs leeks, sliced

1/4 teaspoon caraway seeds
salt and freshly ground black pepper

1. Melt the butter in a large saucepan and gently sauté the leeks until they begin to soften. Mix in the caraway seeds and season with salt and pepper.

2. Spoon onto the opened baked potatoes.

2. Spicy Onion and Carrot

1 lb onions, sliced
2 tablespoons vegetable oil
1/2 lb carrots, grated
2 tablespoons raisins

1 tablespoon tomato purée
1–2 tablespoons soy sauce
freshly ground black pepper

1. In a skillet, fry the onion in the oil until softened. Add the carrots and raisins and stir-fry for 1 minute.

2. Mix together the tomato purée, soy sauce, and pepper, and add it to the vegetables and raisins. Toss again to mix, and heat through.

3. Spoon onto the opened baked potatoes.

3. Blue Cheese and Walnuts

1/2 lb blue cheese (Roquefort, Stilton, or Gorgonzola)
1/8 cup coarsely chopped walnut halves

1-2 tablespoons yogurt or cottage cheese

1. Dice the cheese and mix with the remaining ingredients.

2. Spoon onto the opened baked potatoes.

4. Mushroom and Garlic

3 tablespoons olive oil
2-3 garlic cloves, chopped
1 lb sliced mushrooms

water or wine
salt and freshly ground black pepper
4 tablespoons chopped fresh parsley

1. Heat the oil in a frying pan and fry the garlic. Add the mushrooms and toss over the heat for 2-3 minutes, adding a little water or wine towards the end. Season with salt and pepper.

2. Spoon onto the opened baked potatoes. Serve sprinkled with parsley.

5. Herby Tahini

4 tablespoons tahini
1/2 cup water
freshly ground black pepper

6 tablespoons chopped fresh mixed herbs (chives, parsley, basil, tarragon, or chervil)

1. In a bowl, mix the tahini and water to a smooth creamy texture and stir in the pepper and herbs.

2. Spoon onto the opened baked potatoes.

Spring Rolls

——◆——

All of these Chinese delicacies will probably vanish just as quickly as you can make them. They can be frozen successfully after half the cooking time. To serve later, deep-fry directly from the freezer.

MAKES 12

Filling

1 tablespoon vegetable oil
1 onion, sliced
1 tablespoon chopped fresh ginger
1 garlic clove, crushed
1 carrot, julienned
1/2 cup sliced mushrooms
1 red pepper, seeded and thinly sliced
1/4 lb bean sprouts

1/4 lb bamboo shoots, cut into sticks
1 teaspoon corn flour
salt and freshly ground black pepper
1 teaspoon soy sauce

12 spring roll wrappers
1 egg, beaten
vegetable oil for deep-frying

1. To make the filling, heat the oil in a wok or frying pan and stir-fry the onion, ginger, garlic, and carrot for 2 minutes. Add the mushrooms and pepper, and continue cooking for another 2 minutes. Toss in the bean sprouts and bamboo shoots.

2. Quickly mix together the remaining ingredients and pour into the pan, stirring constantly.

3. Place spoonfuls of the mixture in the center of each spring roll wrapper. Roll up and fold in the ends. Seal with beaten egg and secure with a cocktail pick.

4. Deep-fry the spring rolls in oil for about 3 minutes until they're crisp and golden. Drain and serve.

Vegetable Samosas

——◆——

These little Indian snacks can be made with almost any kind of vegetables. They can be fried in hot oil or baked on a greased tin.

MAKES 8

Filling
1 onion, finely chopped
1 garlic clove, chopped
1 tablespoon vegetable oil
1 tablespoon each garam masala or
    curry powder, and ground cumin
1 teaspoon ground coriander
salt and freshly ground black pepper
4 tablespoons stock (see page x)
1 lb potatoes, peeled and diced
1 cup peas
2 carrots, diced

Pastry
1/2 cup all-purpose flour
pinch of salt
1 teaspoon baking soda
1 tablespoon melted butter
3-3 1/2 teaspoons water

vegetable oil for deep-frying, optional

1. To make the filling, in a saucepan fry the onion and garlic in the oil for 3-4 minutes. Stir in the garam masala (or curry powder), cumin, coriander, salt, pepper, and stock. Add the remaining ingredients and simmer for 20 minutes until the vegetables are cooked and all the liquid has evaporated.

2. To make the pastry, sift the flour, salt, and baking soda into a bowl. Stir in the melted butter and water and knead to an elastic dough.

3. Divide into 8 pieces and roll out each one to make a 4-inch square. Place a tablespoon of filling on each square and fold it over to form a triangle. Dampen the edges of the pastry and pinch together firmly.

4. Deep-fry the triangles in hot oil for 3-4 minutes until golden and slightly bubbly, or bake in an oven preheated to 425°F for 20-30 minutes.

The Main Course

PASTA DISHES

——◆——

Pasta is so quick and simple to prepare that it is featured on my dinner table quite frequently. It's fun to make two toppings if you have the time, but one will do.

The quantities given here are for main-course dishes. Smaller amounts make good starters, and larger quantities can be used as the centerpiece of a hot buffet. Many of the stir-fry dishes in this book can also be served with pasta.

Rigatoni with Goat Cheese and Parsley

——◆——

This dish could hardly be easier to make, but the flavors of the goat cheese, parsley, and olive oil are much more complex than you might expect. I use a hard goat cheese and grate it. Crumble or chop softer cheeses.

12 oz rigatoni
salt
1 teaspoon olive oil
1/2 lb hard goat cheese, grated

2 tablespoons extra-virgin olive oil
4 tablespoons chopped fresh parsley
pinch of dried oregano
freshly ground black pepper

1. Cook the rigatoni as directed on the package in salted boiling water with 1 teaspoon oil.

2. When the pasta is cooked *al dente*, drain and toss with the remaining ingredients. Serve at once.

Fettucini with Sautéed Spring Vegetables

—◆—

This is best made in early summer when the new vegetables are coming into market. At other times of the year, vary the vegetables to suit what's available. This dish makes an unusual starter, but the quantities can be increased and the recipe served as a main course.

8 oz fettucini
salt
2 tablespoons olive oil, divided
2-3 scallions, finely chopped
2-3 new carrots, scrubbed and cut
  into sticks
1/2 lb zucchini, sliced into thin rings

peas or broccoli florets
1 tablespoon chopped fresh parsley
4 tablespoons grated Parmesan cheese
freshly ground black pepper
2 tablespoons pine nuts, toasted
  (see page xi)

1. Cook the fettucini as directed on the package in salted boiling water with 1 teaspoon of the oil. Drain and toss in a little more oil. Keep warm.

2. Heat the remaining oil in a skillet and sauté the scallions and carrots for 3-4 minutes. Add the zucchini and peas or broccoli and continue cooking a few minutes until all the vegetables are tender but still slightly crisp.

3. Spoon the vegetables over the pasta and top with parsley, Parmesan, pine nuts, and black pepper.

Fusilli with Fresh Tomato and Basil Sauce

—◆—

If I can't find good fresh tomatoes, I cheat a little and add some tomato purée. The carrot also adds a certain sweetness.

1 small onion, finely chopped
1-3 garlic cloves, to taste, crushed
2 tablespoons olive oil, divided
1 large carrot, grated
2 lbs tomatoes, peeled (see page xi)
and chopped

1 tablespoon tomato purée
salt and freshly ground black pepper
12 oz fusilli
handful of fresh basil

1. In a skillet, fry the onion and garlic in 5 teaspoons of the oil until lightly browned. Add the carrot and cook 1 more minute. Add the tomatoes and tomato purée and season with salt and pepper. Simmer over low heat for 10 minutes. Rub through a sieve. Keep the mixture warm.

2. Cook the fusilli as directed on the package in salted boiling water with the remaining oil. When it is *al dente*, drain.

3. Tear the basil into small pieces and add to the sauce just before pouring it over the pasta.

Vermicelli D'Abruzzo

—◆—

This is a popular topping for pasta in the Adriatic province of Abruzzo.

12 oz vermicelli
salt
1 teaspoon olive oil
4-5 peppers (red, green, and
yellow mixed)

3 tablespoons extra-virgin olive oil
2 tablespoons capers, well rinsed
freshly ground black pepper
grated Parmesan cheese (optional)

1. Cook the pasta as directed on the package in salted boiling water with the oil. Drain well.

2. Cut the peppers into quarters and remove the seeds. Place skin side up under a hot broiler and broil until the skin is blackened. Place in a bowl and cover with a lid. Peel off and discard the skin after about 15-20 minutes. Cut the flesh into long thin strips.

3. Toss the pasta with the pepper and oil. Serve sprinkled with capers, black pepper, and Parmesan, if desired.

Farfalle with Boursin and Walnut Sauce

—◆—

This is one of the quickest pasta sauces to prepare, with lots of flavor and texture. I like to serve it with bowties, as the sauce seems to collect in delicious quantities in the folds of the pasta.

12 oz farfalle
salt
1 teaspoon olive oil
2 5-oz packages Boursin cheese

1/2 cup light cream
12-14 walnut halves, cut into
quarters
4 tablespoons chopped fresh parsley

1. Cook the farfalle as directed on the package in salted boiling water with the oil. Drain well.

2. Cut the Boursin into chunks and place in a small saucepan with the cream. Heat gently, stirring constantly to produce a smooth creamy sauce. Add the walnuts.

3. Toss the pasta with the sauce. Serve sprinkled with parsley.

Spaghetti with Wild Mushrooms

—◆—

I always keep a supply of dried mushrooms in my pantry. They are expensive, but a very small amount will give a wonderfully strong flavor. Use them on their own for special occasions or mix with button mushrooms for everyday use.

Try to find the sun-dried tomato paste, as it adds such an inimitable flavor.

1 oz dried cèpes
2 heaping tablespoons tomato purée
2 heaping teaspoons sun-dried
 tomato paste
1 onion, finely chopped

2 garlic cloves, crushed
4 teaspoons olive oil, divided
salt and freshly ground black pepper
12 oz spaghetti

1. Place the dried mushrooms in a bowl and just cover with boiling water. Let stand for half an hour. Drain and chop, reserving the liquid to mix with the tomato purée and tomato paste.

2. In a skillet, fry the onion and garlic in 1 tablespoon of the oil until lightly browned. Add the mushrooms and tomato mixture and season with salt and pepper. Bring the mixture to a boil and simmer about 10 minutes, or until the sauce is fairly thick.

3. Cook the spaghetti as directed on the package in salted boiling water with the remaining oil. Drain well.

4. Serve the pasta in bowls with the sauce spooned over it.

Tagliatelle with Pesto Sauce and Black Olives

—◆—

The black olives add an extra dimension to the classic Ligurian pasta with pesto combination. The effect is somehow lighter and less oily, and I find I can eat much more of it. It is essential to use fresh basil.

Pesto sauce
1/2 cup fresh basil leaves
2 garlic cloves
2 tablespoons pine nuts
pinch of salt
2 tablespoons grated Parmesan cheese
1/4 cup olive oil, divided

12 oz tagliatelle
salt
12-14 black olives, pitted and
   cut in half

1. To make the pesto sauce, blend the basil leaves, garlic, and pine nuts in a food processor. Add the salt, cheese, and all but 1 teaspoon of the oil.

2. Cook the tagliatelle as directed on the package in salted boiling water with the remaining oil. When it is *al dente*, drain.

3. Toss the pasta in the pesto sauce. Spoon onto individual plates and top with the olives.

Zucchini with Macaroni

—◆—

Zucchini makes a really juicy accompaniment to macaroni, which can sometimes be rather dry. This quantity makes a good first course.

1 onion, thinly sliced
2 tablespoons olive oil, divided
2 tablespoons butter
1 small zucchini

1 tablespoon chopped fresh basil
1 tablespoon tomato purée
salt and freshly ground black pepper
6 oz macaroni

1. In a skillet, fry the onion in half the oil and the butter until very lightly browned.

2. Dice the zucchini and add it to the saucepan. Continue cooking over low heat, stirring occasionally, until the zucchini just begins to soften. This will take about 5 minutes, depending on the size of the dice. Stir in the basil and tomato purée and season with salt and pepper.

3. Cook the macaroni as directed on the package in salted boiling water. Drain well, and sauté in the remaining oil. Add the zucchini mixture and toss well together. Serve sprinkled with freshly ground black pepper.

Spaghetti with Walnut, Parsley, and Basil Sauce

———◆———

This simple variation on a classic pesto sauce has an excellent flavor of its own. Serve with grated Parmesan or cheddar cheese.

5 tablespoons extra-virgin olive oil, divided
1 large garlic clove, chopped
large handful of fresh parsley, chopped
1/4 cup coarsely ground walnuts
2 tablespoons very hot water
salt and freshly ground black pepper
10-14 fresh basil leaves
1/2 lb spaghetti

1. Heat 2 tablespoons of the oil in a skillet and add the garlic and parsley. Stir over low heat. Add the walnuts and cook for a minute or so, but do not allow them to brown. Stir in all but 1 teaspoon of the remaining oil and the water. Season with salt and pepper and remove from the heat.

2. Cut the basil leaves thinly, stir them into the sauce, and leave in the pan on one side.

3. Cook the spaghetti as directed on the package in salted boiling water with remaining oil. When it is *al dente*, drain, and mix in the sauce.

Spaghetti with Onions and Sun-Dried Tomatoes

——◆——

The combination of the piquancy of the sun-dried tomatoes and the sweetness of the onions is very unusual.

It is important to use freshly grated Parmesan cheese. This cheese keeps well in the refrigerator. Take it out and grate it about an hour before you use it (all cheeses should be served at room temperature).

12 oz spaghetti
salt
2 tablespoons olive oil, divided
1 oz sun-dried tomatoes

2-3 onions, sliced
freshly ground black pepper
freshly grated Parmesan cheese

1. Cook the spaghetti as directed on the package in salted boiling water with 1 teaspoon of the oil. When it is *al dente*, drain.

2. Place the tomatoes in a bowl, cover with boiling water, and let stand for 10-15 minutes.

3. Heat the remaining oil in a small frying pan and fry the onions until they start to brown.

4. Drain the tomatoes and cut them into strips. Toss with the onions.

5. Spoon the onion and tomato over the top of the pasta and season with pepper. Serve with Parmesan cheese.

Tagliatelle with Cannellini Beans

—◆—

This recipe is similar to the *Fettucini al Stufo* which is a specialty of La Spezia, an Italian port on the Mediterranean. The combination of pasta and beans makes a substantial winter dish.

1 1/2 tablespoons olive oil, divided
2 garlic cloves, chopped
1 onion, chopped
3 tablespoons chopped fresh parsley
small handful of fresh rosemary
1/2 cup red wine

1 14-oz can of tomatoes
salt and freshly ground black pepper
1 14-oz can of cannellini beans,
  drained
12 oz tagliatelle

1. Heat a tablespoon of the oil in a skillet and fry the garlic and onion for 2-3 minutes. Add the parsley and rosemary and cook 1 more minute. Pour in the wine and turn up the heat. Boil until half the mixture has evaporated.

2. Add the tomatoes and season with salt and pepper. Cook for 15 minutes, or until the sauce is very thick.

3. Add the beans and cook 5 more minutes.

4. Cook the spaghetti as directed on the package in salted boiling water with the remaining oil. Drain well.

5. Serve the pasta with the bean sauce spooned over the top.

Pasticcio

—◆—

There are both Italian and Greek versions of this macaroni and eggplant pie, but every family there seems to have its own special way of making it. This is a good dish to serve at a buffet party.

SERVES 8-10

2 large eggplants, sliced
salt
8 oz macaroni
1 teaspoon olive oil
1 14-oz can of tomatoes
1 garlic clove, crushed
1 tablespoon tomato purée

2 tablespoons chopped fresh basil
freshly ground black pepper
2 tablespoons butter
2 tablespoons flour
1 cup milk
1 egg, beaten

1. Sprinkle the eggplants with salt and let them stand in a colander weighted down with a plate for at least 30 minutes. Rinse well and squeeze dry.

2. Cook the macaroni as directed on the package in salted boiling water with the oil. Drain well.

3. In a saucepan, place the tomatoes, garlic, tomato purée, basil, salt, and pepper, and bring to a boil. Cook for 10-15 minutes, or until the sauce is fairly thick. Purée in a blender or food processor or rub through a sieve. Mix with the pasta.

4. Preheat the oven to 400°F.

5. Arrange half the eggplant slices in a greased casserole dish and cover with half the pasta. Add another layer of eggplant and another layer of pasta.

6. Place the butter, flour, and milk in a saucepan and bring to a boil, stirring with a wire whisk. When the mixture thickens, remove it from the heat and beat in the egg. Pour over the casserole and bake for 40 minutes.

Penne with Zucchini

—◆—

This zucchini and pasta dish is just as good served chilled as it is hot. I like to serve it hot as a first course, or chilled on a cold buffet. Fresh basil is essential to the flavor.

1 lb zucchini, sliced
4 1/2 tablespoons olive oil, divided
salt and freshly ground black pepper
1/2 cup yogurt

1 teaspoon corn or rice flour
1/2 lb penne
2 tablespoons chopped fresh basil
whole basil leaves

1. In a skillet, fry the zucchini in 4 tablespoons of the oil until very lightly browned. Place in a blender with the salt, pepper, yogurt, and flour, and purée. Return to a saucepan and thicken over low heat, stirring occasionally.

2. Cook the penne as directed on the package in salted boiling water with the remaining oil. Drain well.

3. Stir the basil into the sauce and pour over the top of the pasta. Garnish with whole basil leaves.

Sicilian Pasta

—◆—

This delicious eggplant and mushroom sauce is popular in Sicily. It can be served with any kind of pasta. Marsala, a fortified dessert wine from Sicily, is similar to Oloroso sherry or Madeira.

1 onion, finely chopped
5 tablespoons olive oil, divided
1 eggplant, diced
1 garlic clove, crushed
4 tablespoons chopped fresh parsley

1 tablespoon chopped fresh basil
1/2 lb mushrooms, sliced
1/4 cup Marsala
salt and freshly ground black pepper
12 oz pasta

1. In a skillet, fry the onion in half the oil for 2-3 minutes. Add the eggplant and continue cooking for 8-10 minutes until the eggplant is tender and lightly browned.

2. In another skillet, fry the garlic and herbs in the remaining oil, reserving 1 teaspoon for the pasta water, for 1 minute. Add the mushrooms and fry for 4-5 minutes. Add the Marsala and season with salt and pepper. Increase the heat and boil until most of the liquid has evaporated.

3. Add the onion and eggplant to the mushroom mixture and simmer together for about 2 minutes.

4. Cook the pasta as directed on the package in salted boiling water with the remaining oil. When it is *al dente*, drain. Serve with the sauce.

Lasagne Rolls with Tomato Sauce

—◆—

This is an unusual way to make Italian lasagne—rolling it into wheels. Serve with freshly grated Parmesan cheese.

8 long pieces of lasagne
salt
1 teaspoon vegetable oil
3 lbs fresh spinach, steamed and
  chopped, or 1 lb frozen chopped
  spinach, thawed
12 oz Ricotta cheese
1/2 lb cottage cheese or semi-soft
  low-fat cheese
salt and freshly ground black pepper

Tomato sauce
1 8-oz can of tomatoes
2 cups tomato juice
1/4 teaspoon dried thyme
salt and freshly ground black pepper

freshly grated Parmesan cheese

1. Cook the lasagne as directed on the package in salted boiling water with the oil. Drain and lay out on a piece of wax paper. Cut the lasagne in half lengthwise.

2. Preheat the oven to 400°F.

3. Squeeze out all the liquid from the spinach and mix with the cheeses and salt and pepper. Spread the mixture along the length of each piece of lasagne and roll each one up. Place in a baking dish.

4. To make the sauce, purée the tomatoes in a blender or food processor. Mix with the tomato juice and thyme and season with salt and pepper.

5. Pour into the dish with the lasagne and cover with foil. Bake for about 15 minutes. To serve, sprinkle with a little Parmesan cheese.

RICE AND CEREAL DISHES

The cooking times for rice in this section are based on white rice. If you use the fiber-rich, nutty brown rice available at health-food stores, you will need to extend the cooking time from 12-15 minutes to 30-40 minutes. All the recipes use long-grain rice unless arborio rice is specified.

Some of the rice dishes such as Singapore Rice and Afghan Rice are very good served with a yogurt-based salad such as Raita (see page 169), or simply stir-fry vegetables. Other recipes in this chapter go well with a mixture of dishes. The risottos, too, are very good served on their own with a tossed green salad. Couscous is a meal in itself.

Savory Baked Rice

This dish has lots of texture, flavor, and color, and goes particularly well with all kinds of oriental food.

1/2 cup basmati rice
2 leeks, finely chopped
1 zucchini, finely chopped
4 tablespoons frozen peas
3 tablespoons mixed salted nuts,
  chopped

2 tablespoons chopped apricots
  or raisins
salt and freshly ground black pepper
1 cup boiling water

1. Preheat the oven to 375°F.

2. Mix all the ingredients together and place in a casserole dish. Bake for 45 minutes, or until the rice is tender and all the liquid has been absorbed.

3. Let stand for 5 minutes. Fluff up the rice with a fork before serving.

Singapore Rice

—◆—

The coconut and curry powder contribute to the aromatic flavor of this Malaysian rice dish. Serve with any of the dishes in the stir-fry section (see page 72-83), or as part of a hot buffet.

SERVES 6-8

1 onion, finely chopped
1 small green pepper, seeded and
  finely chopped
2 tablespoons vegetable oil
1/2 teaspoon mild curry powder
1/2 cup coconut cream
1 8-oz can of pineapple slices,
  drained and chopped

2 tablespoons toasted sliced almonds
  (see page xi)
2 tablespoons raisins
1 1/2 cups long-grain rice
3 cups vegetable stock (see page x)
fresh cilantro sprigs

1. In a saucepan, stir-fry the onion and green pepper in the oil. Cook for 2 minutes and then add the remaining ingredients except the cilantro.

2. Bring to a boil. Stir once and cover with a lid. Reduce the heat and cook for 15 minutes, or until the rice is tender and all the liquid has been absorbed.

3. Turn off the heat and let stand for 5 minutes before serving. Garnish with cilantro.

Caribbean Rice

—◆—

The mixed cultural backgrounds of the Caribbean—African, Chinese, and Indian—have all contributed to the flavor of this dish. Try to use limes, as the flavor really is quite different from lemons. The dish can be eaten on its own, but it is also a welcome addition to a hot buffet table.

1 garlic clove, finely chopped
1 onion, finely chopped
1 tablespoon vegetable oil
1 cup long-grain rice
1/4 cup raisins
1 1/2 cups vegetable stock (see page x)
1 tablespoon soy sauce
1 tablespoon toasted sesame oil
1 teaspoon ground turmeric

1 teaspoon minced lime peel
2 tablespoons pine nuts, toasted
  (see page xi)
1/4 green peppers, seeded and cut
  into short strips

Garnishes
sliced lime rind
fresh cilantro leaves

1. In a large saucepan, fry the garlic and onion in the oil for 2 minutes, or until they turn transparent.

2. Add the rice, stir, then add the raisins, stock, soy sauce, sesame oil, turmeric, and minced peel. Bring to a boil, stir, and cover. Reduce the heat and cook 15 more minutes, or until the rice is tender and all the liquid has been absorbed.

3. Let stand for 5 minutes and then stir in the remaining ingredients, retaining a third to sprinkle on top. Garnish with sliced lime rind and cilantro leaves and serve at once.

Curried Rice and Peas

—◆—

Rice and peas is a combination that turns up in countries as diverse as Italy, Jamaica, Brazil, and India. Sometimes the "peas" really are peas, and sometimes they are beans.

1 teaspoon whole cumin seeds
6 black peppercorns
seeds from 3 cardamom pods
2 tablespoons vegetable oil
1 onion, chopped
1 garlic clove, chopped

1 teaspoon garam masala
    or curry powder
1 cup long-grain rice
2 cups water
1 cup cooked peas or canned beans,
    drained
salt and freshly ground black pepper

1. In a saucepan, fry the whole seeds in hot oil for about 1 minute. Add the onion and garlic and continue cooking for 4-5 minutes, or until the onions are lightly browned.

2. Stir in the curry powder and rice, making sure that the rice is well coated with oil and spices. Pour in the water, and bring to a boil. Stir once and cover with a lid. Simmer for 12-15 minutes.

3. Stir in the peas or beans and season with salt and pepper. Cook for a few more minutes, or until the rice is tender and all the liquid has been absorbed. Let stand for 3-5 minutes before serving.

Eggplant Pilau

—◆—

This interesting spiced dish from Saudi Arabia is excellent served with vegetable kebabs or satay and salad.

1/4 teaspoon whole mustard seeds or cumin seeds
1/2 teaspoon poppy seeds
2 whole cloves
1/2 teaspoon ground turmeric
1/4 teaspoon ground cinnamon
1 tablespoon ground almonds

3 tablespoons butter or 1 tablespoon oil and 2 tablespoons butter
1 eggplant, peeled and diced
1 onion, finely chopped
1 cup long-grain rice
1 1/2 cups water
salt

1. In a saucepan, fry the spices and almonds in the butter or the mixture of butter and oil. After a few minutes, add the diced eggplant and stir well. Add the onion and continue to fry for about 5 minutes, stirring regularly.

2. Add the rice and stir, making sure that it is well mixed in. Pour in the water and season with salt. Bring to a boil and reduce the heat. Cover and simmer for 15 minutes, or until the rice is tender and all the liquid has been absorbed.

3. Turn off the heat and leave for 5 minutes. Fluff up the rice with a fork before serving.

Afghan Rice

———◆———

This well-flavored rice dish is very good eaten on its own with Raita (see page 169) and salad. The presence of the curry powder and cinnamon reveals influences of both the Far East and the Middle East.

3 tablespoons pine nuts
1 onion, finely chopped
2 tablespoons vegetable oil
1 cup long-grain rice
2 cups vegetable stock (see page x)

1 small packet of saffron
2 tablespoons raisins
pinch of mild curry powder
1 cinnamon stick

1. Toast the pine nuts in a hot oven to brown them lightly. Set aside.

2. In a saucepan, fry the onion in the oil for about 5-6 minutes, or until lightly browned.

3. Add the rice and stir, making sure that it is well coated with oil. Add the stock and the remaining ingredients. Bring the mixture to a boil. Stir once and cover with a lid. Reduce the heat and simmer for 15 minutes, or until the rice is tender and all the liquid has been absorbed.

4. Turn off the heat and let stand for 3-4 minutes. Fluff up the rice with a fork before serving.

Texan Rice

This recipe comes from a Texan friend who refers to it as Mexican Rice. However, the genuine Mexican version is probably hotter than this mild but delicious dish.

2 tablespoons vegetable oil
1 green chile, seeded and
   finely chopped
pinch of saffron
1 cup long-grain rice
1 14-oz can of tomatoes
1/2 cup water

2 red onions, cut into rings
1 red pepper, seeded and cut
   into rings
1 green pepper, seeded and cut
   into rings
salt and freshly ground black pepper

1. Heat the oil in a saucepan and fry the chile and saffron about 2 minutes.

2. Add the rice and continue frying and stirring until the rice is very lightly browned. Add the tomatoes and water. Stir once and bring to a boil.

3. Arrange the onion and pepper rings on top and season with salt and pepper. Cover with a lid and cook over low heat for 30 minutes, or until the rice and vegetables are tender and all the liquid has been absorbed. Serve at once without stirring.

Red Bean Risotto

———◆———

The red beans add color and flavor to this Italian rice dish, but if you do not have a can handy, simply substitute more peas.

1 small onion, chopped
2 garlic cloves, chopped
1 green pepper, seeded and chopped
4 tablespoons butter or
  3 tablespoons olive oil
1 1/2 cups Italian arborio rice
1 cup dry white wine
1 teaspoon dried mixed herbs

2 cups vegetable stock (see page x)
salt and freshly ground black pepper
4 tablespoons frozen peas
1 cup canned red beans, drained
3 tablespoons chopped fresh mixed
  herbs (basil, tarragon, parsley,
  and chervil)

1. In a saucepan, sauté the onion, garlic, and green pepper in butter or oil until softened.

2. Add the rice and fry for 3-4 minutes. Add the wine and bring to a boil. Continue cooking until all the wine is absorbed, stirring occasionally.

3. Add the dried mixed herbs and stock and season with salt and pepper. Continue cooking for 20-30 minutes, or until the rice is tender. Add more stock if the rice is too dry.

4. Add the frozen peas, beans, and fresh herbs. Heat through and serve at once.

Millet and Lentil Pilau

—◆—

I like to serve this dish with Roman-Style Spinach (see page 77) and a spicy onion and tomato salad, perhaps with a little sour cream or yogurt.

1 cup millet
1 tablespoon vegetable oil
1 teaspoon cumin seeds
1 small onion, finely chopped

1 garlic clove, crushed
1/2 cup split lentils
1 teaspoon ground coriander
2 cups vegetable stock (see page x)

1. Fry the millet in a hot nonstick frying pan until lightly browned. Remove the millet from the pan and set aside.

2. Heat the oil in the same pan and fry the cumin seeds for 1 minute. Add the onion and garlic and fry until lightly browned.

3. Stir in the lentils, millet, and coriander. Add the stock and bring to a boil. Stir and cover with a lid. Reduce the heat and simmer for 30 minutes. Check to see if more liquid is required, stir, and continue cooking for 10-15 more minutes, or until the millet and lentils are fully cooked.

4. Let stand for 5 minutes with the lid on. Fluff up the millet with a fork before serving.

Mushroom and Walnut Risotto

——◆——

This unusually flavored risotto is a vegan's dream, as it really is much nicer without the usually obligatory Parmesan cheese. It is important to use Italian arborio rice.

3 tablespoons olive oil, divided
1 small onion, sliced, divided
1/2 lb button mushrooms, sliced
1 green apple, cored and sliced
8 walnuts, quartered

1/2 cup dry white wine
1 cup Italian risotto rice
2 cups vegetable stock (see page x)
salt and freshly ground black pepper

1. Heat 2 tablespoons of the oil in a large saucepan and fry a quarter portion of the onion, the mushrooms, apple, and walnuts for 2-3 minutes. Add the wine and cook for 10 minutes. Drain off the wine and reserve. Remove the vegetables, apple, and nuts from the pan and keep warm.

2. Put the remaining oil in the saucepan and fry the remaining onion for 2 minutes. Add the rice and sauté for 2 minutes, stirring constantly. Add the reserved wine and boil until it evaporates, stirring the rice occasionally.

3. Add the stock and cook without stirring for 25-30 minutes, or until all the liquid has been absorbed.

4. Stir in the reserved onions, mushrooms, apples, and walnuts. Season with salt and pepper and serve.

Green Risotto

——◆——

This colorful risotto from the plains of Lombardy is delicious served with grated Romano cheese.

2 tablespoons olive oil
2 leeks, sliced
1 lb Swiss chard, shredded
1 small bunch parsley, chopped

1 cup Italian arborio rice
salt and freshly ground black pepper
2 1/2 cups very hot vegetable stock
(see page x)

1. Heat the oil in a pan and fry the leeks, Swiss chard, and parsley for 5 minutes, stirring occasionally.

2. Add the rice and season with salt and pepper. Add a ladle of stock. Cook over low to medium heat until the liquid is almost evaporated, stirring occasionally.

3. Add another ladle of stock. Cook until almost evaporated. Repeat this process, adding more stock, cooking, and stirring occasionally, until the rice is cooked but still firm. Cook off any remaining liquid. The risotto should be slightly creamy but not wet. Total cooking time after adding the rice will be about 30-35 minutes.

Bulgur and Rice

—◆—

The bulgur wheat gives an interesting texture to this mixed grain dish. Serve it with any of the stir-fry or casserole dishes (see pages 72-83 and 84-102).

3/4 cup long-grain rice
1/2 cup bulgur
2 cups vegetable stock (see page x)
salt

2 tablespoons crushed peanuts
2 tablespoons olive oil
2 tablespoons chopped fresh chives

1. Wash the rice and bulgur and drain. Bring the stock to a boil and add the rice, bulgur, and salt. Stir once, cover, and simmer for 40-45 minutes, or until the rice is tender and all the liquid has been absorbed. Turn off the heat and let stand for 10 minutes. Fluff the rice with a fork before serving.

2. In a skillet, fry the nuts in the oil until well browned and sprinkle them over the bulgur and rice with the chives. Serve at once.

North African Couscous

—◆—

Like pasta, couscous is made from fine semolina, which is mixed with water and made into very small pellets. In North Africa, couscous is steamed over vegetables in a special pot. Elsewhere it is easier to steam by itself in a steamer or in a sieve over a pan of boiling water.

1 cup couscous
1 1/2 cups warm water
1 cup vegetable stock (see page x)
4 carrots, cut into sticks
12 small onions
4 turnips

1 14 1/2-oz can of chickpeas, drained
1/2 cup frozen peas
1/4 cup raisins
1 1/2 teaspoons ground allspice
1 teaspoon ground cumin
salt and freshly ground black pepper

1. Soak the couscous in a bowl with warm water for 10 minutes while you prepare the vegetables.

2. Place the stock in a saucepan and add the carrots, onions, and turnips. Simmer for 15 minutes.

3. Add the chickpeas, peas, raisins, allspice, cumin, salt, and pepper. Cook for 15 more minutes.

4. Meanwhile, steam the couscous for 20-30 minutes with a lid on top, making sure that the water does not touch the steamer or the couscous will get lumpy.

5. Stir the cooked couscous with a fork before turning it out onto a large warmed plate. Make a well in the center and spoon in the vegetable mixture.

Vegetable Tagine

—◆—

A tagine is a spicy stew from Morocco containing dried fruit. It is also the name of the pot in which the stew is cooked.

SERVES 6

1 cup couscous
1 1/2 cups warm water
2 tablespoons olive oil
2 onions, quartered
2 garlic cloves, crushed
3 carrots, sliced
2 parsnips, diced
1 teaspoon paprika
1/2 teaspoon each of ground ginger and cinnamon
1 teaspoon each of ground turmeric and coriander
1/4 lb button mushrooms
2 zucchini, sliced

1/4 lb green beans, cut into 2-inch lengths
2 1/2 cups vegetable stock (see page x)
4 tomatoes, peeled (see page xi), seeded, and quartered
1 15-oz can artichoke hearts, drained and halved
1 15-oz can cannellini beans, drained and rinsed
1/4 lb pitted California prunes
2 tablespoons each of chopped fresh parsley and cilantro
2 teaspoons honey or to taste
salt and freshly ground black pepper

1. Soak the couscous in a bowl with the warm water for 10 minutes while you prepare the vegetables.

2. Steam the couscous for 20-30 minutes with a lid on top, making sure that the water does not touch the steamer or the couscous will get lumpy.

3. Meanwhile, heat the oil in a large saucepan and add the onions, garlic, carrots, and parsnips. Fry for 10 minutes, then stir in the spices and cook for 1 more minute.

4. Add the mushrooms, zucchini, green beans, and stock. Bring to a boil, then cook for 10 minutes. Add the tomatoes, artichoke hearts, cannellini beans, prunes, and herbs. Cook for 10 more minutes, or until the vegetables are tender. Add the honey and season with salt and pepper.

5. Stir the cooked couscous with a fork before turning it out onto 4 individual warm plates. Make a well in the center and spoon in the vegetable mixture.

Dry-Fried Okra with Bulgur

—◆—

Unlike some dishes using okra, the result here is quite dry. No liquid is added to the dish and any stickiness from the sliced okra seems to be absorbed by the bulgur. Add 1/2 cup cooked fava beans at the last minute for a more substantial dish. If you like to have a sauce with your food, serve with one of the stir-fry or casserole dishes (see pages 72-83 and 84-102).

1/4 cup bulgur
1 tablespoon vegetable oil
3 scallions, finely chopped

1 red pepper, seeded and
  very finely chopped
3/4 lb okra, thinly sliced
salt and freshly ground black pepper

1. Cover the bulgur with cold water and let stand for 30 minutes. Drain and dry thoroughly on paper towels.

2. Heat the oil in a wok or frying pan and fry the scallions and pepper for 1 minute. Add the okra and continue to stir-fry for another 2 minutes.

3. Add the dried bulgur and season with salt and pepper. Toss over very high heat until the bulgur begins to brown slightly. Serve at once.

Baked Barley with Mushrooms

— ◆ —

This recipe uses whole-grain barley. It is not designed for pearl barley, which has little nutrient value anyway.

2 tablespoons vegetable oil
1 large onion, finely chopped
1 carrot, grated
1/2 lb button mushrooms, sliced
3/4 cup barley, washed and drained

1 cup vegetable stock (see page x)
1/2 teaspoon dried marjoram
or oregano
salt and freshly ground black pepper

1. Preheat the oven to 350°F.

2. Heat the oil in a casserole dish and fry the onion for 2-3 minutes. Add the carrot and mushrooms and continue cooking for another 3-4 minutes, or until the vegetables begin to soften.

3. Stir in the barley, then add the remaining ingredients and bake, covered, for 1 hour, or until the barley is cooked through.

STIR-FRY DISHES

In China, stir-frying is a very quick process that does not use much fat. The temperatures are very high and difficult to reproduce at home. The answer is to use a nonstick wok with no more than a couple of tablespoons of oil. It is actually possible to stir-fry with no oil at all, but in 3-4 tablespoons of stock. If you try this, keep the heat turned up to high to boil off the liquid.

Most of the dishes in this section are very quick to prepare. They can be served with rice or Chinese noodles, but they also make a good topping for pasta or a filling for baked potatoes.

I like to serve two or three dishes at once, which looks attractive and adds interest to the plate. As a result, the quantities given here are based on the idea that at least two dishes will be served at once. If you only have time to make one dish, the quantities will serve two hungry people.

Gujerati Cabbage

This very quick spicy vegetable dish is served as an everyday item in the Indian state of Gujerat. Any kind of cabbage can be used.

2 tablespoons vegetable oil
1 teaspoon whole cumin seeds
1 teaspoon whole black or yellow mustard seeds
1 onion, sliced
1 cup green or white cabbage, finely chopped
1/2 cup red cabbage, finely chopped

1/2 cup carrots, coarsely grated
1/2 small fresh green chile, seeded and cut into very thin strips
1/2 teaspoon salt
pinch of sugar
2 heaping tablespoons chopped fresh cilantro
1 tablespoon lemon juice

1. Heat the oil in a wok or deep-frying pan and fry the whole cumin and mustard seeds until they begin to pop.

2. Quickly add the onion, cabbage, carrots, and green chile. Reduce the heat and stir-fry the vegetables for 5 minutes.

3. Add the remaining ingredients except the lemon juice and cook for 10 more minutes, covered, stirring occasionally.

4. Just before serving, pour on the lemon juice and toss the vegetables.

Zucchini with Pine Nuts and Orange

—— ◆ ——

The zucchini take up the flavor of the orange very well. Serve with Fava Beans in Tahini Sauce or Leeks with Cashew Nuts (see page 75).

6-8 scallions, chopped
2 tablespoons olive oil
1 lb zucchini, sliced
3 tablespoons pine nuts, toasted
  (see page xi)

juice and finely grated rind of
  1 large orange
1 tablespoon chopped fresh dill
salt and freshly ground black pepper

1. In a wok or deep-frying pan, fry the scallions in oil for 1 minute. Add the zucchini and stir-fry for 2 minutes.

2. Add the remaining ingredients, and toss over high heat until most of the juice has evaporated. Serve at once.

Tofu with Cashew Nuts

—◆—

It is worth remembering that tofu is a good substitute for dairy food. It behaves in much the same way, but contains no saturated fat. Any kind of vegetables in season can be used in this recipe. Good alternative combinations include sugar snap peas with sweet corn and carrots; green peppers with bamboo shoots; and fennel or broccoli with red chile peppers and celery root.

2 tablespoons vegetable oil, divided
1 garlic clove, finely chopped
3 teaspoons grated fresh ginger, divided
1/2 lb tofu, cut into strips
1/2 bunch scallions, cut into lengths
2 carrots, cut into thin sticks
1/4 lb string beans

1 8-oz can of water chestnuts, drained and sliced
3 tablespoons vegetable stock (see page x)
1 tablespoon soy sauce
2 tablespoons cashew nuts, toasted (see page xi)
1 tablespoon pine nuts, toasted (see page xi)

1. Heat 1 tablespoon of the oil in a wok or deep-frying pan and fry the garlic and half the ginger.

2. Add the tofu and carefully stir-fry for about 1 minutes, then remove it from the pan.

3. Add the remaining oil and ginger to the pan with all the vegetables and the water chestnuts. Stir-fry for 2-3 minutes.

4. Pour in the stock and soy sauce and toss over high heat for 1 minute. Reduce the heat and cook, covered, for 1-2 more minutes.

5. Add the cashew nuts, pine nuts, and tofu, and toss over low heat. Serve at once.

Fava Beans in Tahini Sauce

—◆—

Tahini is a paste of crushed sesame seeds in their own oil. It usually needs to be diluted with lemon juice or water. The longer you cook this sauce, the thicker it will become. One minute in the wok or pan should be sufficient to heat it through without thickening it too much.

3/4 lb fresh or frozen fava beans
6-8 scallions, chopped
1 tablespoon vegetable oil

3 tablespoons tahini
1/2 cup water
salt and freshly ground black pepper

1. Cook the beans in salted boiling water until just tender.

2. In a wok or deep-frying pan, stir-fry the scallions in the oil for 1 minute. Add the beans and toss well together.

3. Gradually mix the tahini with the water to form a smooth cream. Season with salt and pepper, then pour over the beans and heat through.

Leeks with Cashew Nuts

—◆—

The flavor of leeks merges well with that of the celery in this easy-to-prepare dish. Serve with pasta spirals and one other sauce or topping.

1 large head of celery, sliced
3-4 leeks, sliced
1/4 garlic clove, chopped
2 tablespoons olive oil

3 tablespoons cashew nuts, toasted
(see page xi)
2 tablespoons chopped fresh parsley
1 tablespoon chopped fresh basil
salt and freshly ground black pepper

1. In a wok or deep-frying pan, stir-fry the celery, leeks, and garlic in the oil for 2-3 minutes.

2. Add the remaining ingredients. Toss well to heat through. Serve at once.

Spiced Yams

— ◆ —

This is a variation on a Spanish recipe for spiced potatoes. It is very good made with both regular and sweet potatoes as well as with yams.

1 1/2 lbs yams, peeled and cubed
1 teaspoon lemon juice
1 onion, finely chopped
1 tablespoon vegetable oil

3 red chile peppers, seeded
  and chopped
1/2 teaspoon ground allspice
pinch of ground nutmeg
salt and freshly ground black pepper

1. Cook the yams with the lemon juice in salted boiling water for about 15 minutes until tender. Drain well.

2. Meanwhile, in a wok or deep-frying pan fry the onion in the oil until lightly browned.

3. Add the remaining ingredients and the yams. Fry for 3-4 minutes, turning occasionally.

Stir-Fried Broccoli with Tofu

— ◆ —

This oriental recipe uses purple sprouting broccoli rather than the more compact Calabrese.

2 oz slivered almonds
1 tablespoon vegetable oil
1 onion, thinly sliced
1 lb purple sprouting broccoli,
  washed and cut into lengths

1/4 lb tofu, diced
1 tablespoon soy sauce
pinch of five-spice powder

1. Toast the slivered almonds in a dry frying pan to brown them. Remove the almonds from the pan and set aside.

2. Add the oil to the pan and stir-fry the onion for 1 minute. Add the broccoli and continue stir-frying for 2 more minutes.

3. Add the tofu, soy sauce, and five-spice powder and cook another minute. Serve at once. The broccoli should still be crunchy.

Roman-Style Spinach

——◆——

I love this dish simply served with rice or pasta, but it can also be used to accompany a variety of other dishes. It is really important to squeeze out as much liquid as possible from the cooked spinach before stir-frying it, otherwise it will be watery.

1 1/2 lbs spinach
1 garlic clove, roughly sliced
3 tablespoons olive oil
2 tablespoons pine nuts

2 tablespoons raisins, soaked in warm water for 15 minutes and drained
salt and freshly ground black pepper

1. Wash the spinach well, then cook in a large pan with no added water. Squeeze dry.

2. In a wok or deep-frying pan, fry the garlic and pine nuts in the oil until browned. Set aside.

3. Toss the spinach and raisins in the oil until well coated and then add the pine nuts. Toss over heat for 3-4 minutes, season with salt and pepper, and serve.

Beets with Dill

—◆—

Beets take well to other strong flavors. I vary this recipe depending on my mood, sometimes adding 1/2 teaspoon grated orange rind or garlic or whole cumin seeds.

1 tablespoon vegetable oil
1/2 teaspoon grated orange rind,
  crushed garlic, or whole cumin
  seeds (optional)

2 large cooked beets, peeled and diced
4 tablespoons yogurt
6-8 fresh dill sprigs
salt and freshly ground black pepper

1. Heat the oil in a wok or deep-frying pan and fry either the orange rind, garlic, or cumin seeds, if desired.

2. Add the beets and toss in the oil for 2-3 minutes.

3. Add the remaining ingredients and toss over fairly high heat until the sauce thickens.

Stir-Fried Mixed Beans

—◆—

This dish is both colorful and tasty. Other kinds of beans can be substituted, depending on the contents of your cupboards and the fresh beans on sale.

1 small onion, finely chopped
1 garlic clove, crushed (optional)
2 tablespoons peanut oil
1/2 lb string beans, cut into lengths
1/2 lb fava beans
1/4 lb canned red kidney beans,
  drained

4 tablespoons vegetable stock
  (see page x)
1/2 teaspoon grated lemon rind
2 tablespoons fresh chopped parsley
salt and freshly ground black pepper

1. In a wok or deep-frying pan, fry the onion and garlic in the oil for 2 minutes, then add the string beans and fava beans. Stir-fry for 2-3 minutes.

2. Add the remaining ingredients. Bring to a boil and cook over high heat 1-2 more minutes, stirring constantly.

String Beans with Feta Cheese

—◆—

Most cheeses cannot be used in stir-fry because they melt and get stringy. Feta is better since it tends to stiffen with heat.

3 tablespoons vegetable oil, divided
dash of toasted sesame oil
3/4 lb string beans, sliced
2 leeks, sliced

1/4 lb feta cheese, broken into pieces
freshly ground black pepper
1 teaspoon sesame seeds, toasted
  (see page xi)

1. Heat 2 tablespoons of the vegetable oil with the sesame oil in a wok or deep-frying pan, and stir-fry the beans for 2 minutes. Add the leeks and continue cooking for another 1-2 more minutes.

2. Heat the remaining oil and stir-fry the cheese for about 1 minute.

3. Return the vegetables to the pan and toss with the cheese. Serve sprinkled with pepper and sesame seeds.

Greek Cheese Squares with Olives

—◆—

I often serve this colorful chunky mixture on large pieces of toasted Greek or Italian bread.

2 tablespoons vegetable oil
6 scallions, finely chopped
1 garlic clove, crushed
6 oz feta cheese, cut into squares
12-16 black olives, pitted

pinch of dried thyme or oregano
4 tomatoes, cut into wedges or
 coarsely chopped
4 tablespoons chopped fresh basil
salt and freshly ground black pepper

1. Heat the oil in a wok or deep-frying pan and stir-fry the scallions and garlic for 1 minute.

2. Add the remaining ingredients and toss over medium heat for about another minute. Serve as soon as the tomatoes have warmed through.

Mixed Root Vegetable Sticks in Soy Sauce

—◆—

The secret of this simple dish is to combine the vegetables with complementary flavors. The ginger, sherry, and soy go well with root vegetables. I also like to use beets and rutabagas or parsnips and carrots.

3 tablespoons vegetable oil
1 scallion, finely sliced
1 garlic clove
1 teaspoon grated fresh ginger
1 large potato, peeled and cut into
 thin sticks

1/2 medium celery root, peeled and
 cut into thin sticks
2 carrots, cut into thin sticks
4 tablespoons vegetable stock
 (see page x)
1 tablespoon soy sauce
freshly ground black pepper

1. Heat the oil in a wok or deep-frying pan and stir-fry the scallion, garlic, and ginger for 2 minutes.

2. Add the potato and cook for another 2 minutes.

3. Add the other vegetables and continue stir-frying for 2-3 minutes.

4. Add the remaining ingredients and bring to a boil. Cover with a lid and cook for 2-3 more minutes, stirring occasionally, or until the potato is cooked through and most of the liquid has evaporated.

Fried Noodles

——◆——

Fried noodles make a change from rice and can be served with any of the stir-fried dishes in this chapter. They also make a good dish in their own right if you add one or two of the flavorings suggested below. Prepare any chosen flavoring in advance.

1/2 lb Chinese egg noodles　　　　*1 teaspoon soy sauce*
3-4 tablespoons vegetable oil　　　　*freshly ground black pepper*

1. Cook the noodles as directed on the package. Drain well before frying.

2. Heat the oil in a wok or deep-frying pan and add the noodles. Stir-fry for 1 minute. Add the soy sauce and pepper and toss well. If you are using some of the flavorings prepared in advance, add them at this stage.

Suggested Flavorings

1 red pepper, seeded, cut into strips, and stir-fried with 1 tablespoon toasted almonds (see page xi)

or

1/2 bunch watercress with the segments of 1 orange, chopped, and 1 teaspoon sesame seeds

or

1/2 lb zucchini, diced, stir-fried with 1 teaspoon chopped fresh ginger

Noodles with Indonesian Sauce

—◆—

This tasty, peanut-flavored noodle dish is quick to prepare and fun to eat. Serve with a spicy chutney and green salad.

Sauce

3 tablespoons peanut butter
3/4 cup hot water
1 teaspoon black molasses
2 tablespoons soy sauce
1/2 garlic clove, crushed
3 tablespoons lemon juice

1/2 lb Chinese dried egg noodles
2 tablespoons vegetable oil

1 tablespoon grated fresh ginger
2 onions, sliced
1 large red or green pepper, seeded
  and sliced
3/4 lb bok choy, sliced
1/4 lb bean sprouts
3 tablespoons salted peanuts
1 tablespoon soy sauce

1. To make the sauce, mix the peanut butter with the hot water. Stir in the remaining ingredients and bring to a boil. Stir and keep warm.

2. Plunge the noodles into boiling water and turn off the heat. Let stand for 5 minutes. Drain well.

3. Heat the oil in a wok or deep-frying pan and quickly stir-fry the ginger and onions. Add the pepper and continue to stir-fry for 2-3 minutes. Add the bok choy, bean sprouts, and peanuts. Toss over the heat for 2-3 more minutes. The vegetables should soften but remain crisp in the center.

4. Toss the noodles with the vegetables, sprinkle on the soy sauce, and serve with the peanut sauce.

Fresh Ratatouille

———◆———

Ratatouille is one of the most popular Mediterranean vegetable dishes. This fresh-tasting version includes fava beans. Serve with rice or bulgur wheat.

1 tablespoon olive oil
1/2 lb onions, chopped
1 clove garlic, crushed
1 red pepper, seeded and chopped
1 yellow pepper, seeded and chopped
1 eggplant, chopped

1/4 lb zucchini, sliced
2 tablespoons tomato purée
1/2 cup dry white wine
salt and freshly ground black pepper
1/4 lb fava beans

1. Heat the oil in a wok or deep-frying pan and fry all the vegetables except the fava beans for 3-4 minutes.

2. Add the tomato purée and wine and season with salt and pepper. Cook for about 15 minutes, then add the fava beans, and cook 10 more minutes. Serve at once.

CASSEROLES

—◆—

This section contains a collection of dishes that are baked in the oven or stewed on the stovetop. Many of them are quick to prepare, and you can do other things while they cook. Dishes like Potato Stew, Russian Cabbage Pie, Tortino di Zucchini, Malaysian Vegetable-Fruit Curry, Vegetarian Chili, African Curried Vegetables, and Fennel Bean Pot only need the addition of rice, potatoes, bulgur, or bread to complete the meal.

Other dishes can be baked together or served with dishes from other sections of this book. Ideas are given in the menu planning section on pages xi-xii.

Potato Stew

—◆—

This is a favorite winter dish from my childhood. My mother would serve steaming bowls of it topped with a mixture of freshly grated carrot and cheese.

3 onions, sliced
2 tablespoons vegetable oil
4-5 tablespoons rolled oatmeal
2 1/2 cups vegetable stock (see page x)

1 heaping tablespoon nutritional yeast
4-6 large potatoes, peeled and cut into chunks
salt and freshly ground black pepper

1. In a large saucepan, fry the onions in the oil until golden.

2. Add the oatmeal and continue cooking for a few minutes. Add the stock and yeast and bring to a boil.

3. Add the potatoes and season with salt and pepper. Simmer for 30 minutes, stirring occasionally, or until the potatoes are cooked. Add a little more stock if the stew gets too thick.

Spiced Potatoes

—◆—

These delicately spiced potatoes go with all kinds of food, not just Indian food. Yogurt generally requires the addition of flour to prevent it from separating in cooking. This isn't necessary here because most of the liquid evaporates during cooking.

1 tablespoon vegetable oil
1 teaspoon whole cumin seeds
1/2 teaspoon curry powder
1/4 teaspoon ground bay leaf

1/4 teaspoon celery salt
freshly ground black pepper
1 1/2 lbs potatoes, peeled and cubed
1/2 cup yogurt

1. Heat the oil in a large saucepan and fry the cumin seeds for about 1 minute. Add the curry, bay leaf, celery salt, and pepper and fry a few more minutes.

2. Add the potatoes, stirring to make sure that they are well coated with the spices.

3. Pour on the yogurt, stir, and bring to a boil. Cover and simmer for 20-30 minutes, stirring occasionally, or until the potatoes are tender and most of the liquid has been absorbed.

Baked Sweet Potatoes

———◆———

This specialty from the Deep South has a sweet flavor that goes well with Russian Cabbage Pie or Artichokes Jerusalem (see pages 87 and 91).

4 small sweet potatoes
4 tablespoons butter
2 tablespoons brown sugar
pinch of salt
1 tablespoon sherry

1 8-oz can of pineapple slices, drained
1/4 teaspoon grated nutmeg
2 tablespoons raisins

1. Preheat the oven to 375°F.

2. Bake the sweet potatoes for about a half hour until tender. Cut the potatoes in half, scoop out the flesh, and mash with a fork.

3. Place the butter, sugar, salt, and sherry in a saucepan and heat, stirring constantly. When the sugar has dissolved and the butter melted, add the pineapple, nutmeg, and raisins.

4. Mix with the mashed potato. Spoon the mixture back into the potato skins, return to the oven, and bake in a casserole dish for 10 minutes.

Braised Cabbage with Grapefruit

———◆———

This unusual combination of flavors works very well. The recipe comes from an old cookbook belonging to my grandmother.

1/2 large green Savoy cabbage, shredded
2 Granny Smith apples, peeled, cored, and chopped

juice of 1 grapefruit
3/4 cup yogurt
salt and freshly ground black pepper

1. Preheat the oven to 400°F.

2. Mix the cabbage and apples together and place them in a casserole dish. Pour the grapefruit over the top, cover, and bake for 45 minutes.

3. Stir in the yogurt and season with salt and pepper. Cover again, and continue cooking 15 more minutes.

Russian Cabbage Pie

—◆—

This pie, flavored with caraway and cardamom, can be topped with pastry instead of mashed potatoes.

1/2 teaspoon caraway seeds
seeds from 4 cardamom pods
1 cup sour cream
4 tablespoons butter, divided
2 lbs white cabbage, finely shredded

salt and freshly ground black pepper
1/2 lb cooked beets
4 hard-boiled eggs, sliced
1 1/2 lbs potatoes, peeled and cooked
milk

1. Crush the caraway and cardamom seeds together in a mortar and pestle. Mix with the sour cream and set aside.

2. Melt 2 tablespoons of the butter in a large saucepan and add the cabbage. Fry for 3-4 minutes until the cabbage softens. Pour in the spiced sour cream mixture and season with salt and pepper. Cover with a lid and cook over low heat for 40 minutes, stirring occasionally.

3. Meanwhile, preheat the oven to 400°F.

4. Mix the beets with the cabbage and transfer the mixture to a casserole dish. Arrange a layer of hard-boiled egg slices over the top and add a little more salt and pepper. Mash the potatoes with the remaining butter and a little milk, and spread over the dish, making an attractive pattern on the top with a fork. Bake for 15-20 minutes.

Cabbage Lorraine

—◆—

The French province of Lorraine borders on Germany, sharing many German culinary traditions. Here the caraway seeds, popular in Germany, are used with a French accent. The recipe can also be made using bok choy.

1 small or 1/2 large cabbage,
   cut into wedges
salt
1 small onion, sliced
2 tablespoons butter
2 tomatoes, peeled (see page xi)
   and chopped

large pinch of caraway seeds
1 tablespoon flour
1 cup vegetable stock (see page x)
   or water
freshly ground black pepper
3 tablespoons sour cream
1 tablespoon chopped fresh parsley

1. Preheat the oven to 350°F.

2. Blanch the wedges of cabbage in lightly salted boiling water for 7-8 minutes. Place in a casserole dish.

3. In a large saucepan, fry the onion in the butter until very lightly browned. Add the tomatoes and continue frying for a few minutes. Stir in the caraway seeds, flour, and stock. Continue cooking and stirring until the mixture thickens.

4. Season with salt and pepper, then pour the sauce over the cabbage. Bake for 45 minutes, basting occasionally.

5. Pour the sour cream over the top and bake another 15 minutes. Serve sprinkled with parsley.

Cabbage and Onion Casserole

—◆—

Any kind of cabbage can be used for this substantial vegetable casserole. Turn it into a main course by adding 1/3 cup uncooked rice and 3 tablespoons vegetable stock to the mix, and serve it with plenty of grated cheese sprinkled over each portion.

1 lb cabbage, shredded
3 large onions, sliced
1 leek, sliced (optional)
4 tablespoons butter

2 tablespoons chopped fresh mint
* or dill, or 1/4 teaspoon cumin*
caraway seeds
salt and freshly ground black pepper

1. Preheat the oven to 375°F.

2. Layer the vegetables in a casserole dish, adding a few pats of butter and a sprinkling of herbs and spices to each layer. Finish with a layer of cabbage.

3. Cover with a lid and bake for about 1 hour, or until the vegetables are tender.

Braised Red Cabbage

—◆—

The oranges and raisins in this recipe complement the red cabbage well, giving an unusual flavor to the finished dish.

1 onion, sliced
1 tablespoon vegetable oil
1 lb red cabbage, finely shredded
2 tablespoons raisins

juice and finely grated rind of
* 1 orange*
2 tablespoons red currant jelly
2 tablespoons cider vinegar

1. In a large saucepan, fry the onion in the oil for about 4-5 minutes, or until softened and lightly browned.

2. Add the cabbage and continue cooking, stirring occasionally, for 10 more minutes.

3. Mix the remaining ingredients and add them to the pan. Stir well and bring to a boil. Cover and simmer for 45-50 minutes, or until the cabbage is tender and most of the liquid has been absorbed.

Stewed Beets with Onions

——◆——

Beets are one of my favorite vegetables. I particularly like them spicy. This recipe is quite spicy, but if you prefer something a little milder, use the juice and rind of 1 orange in place of the cumin, garlic, and tomato purée. Use cooked beets for a speedier result; this cuts the cooking time to 15-20 minutes.

2 tablespoons vegetable oil
1 teaspoon whole cumin seeds
1 garlic clove, crushed
2 onions, sliced
salt and freshly ground black pepper

1 lb small beets, peeled and cut
  into wedges
2 tablespoons tomato purée
juice of 1 lemon
1/4 cup water

1. Heat the oil in a large saucepan and fry the cumin seeds and garlic for 1 minute. Add the onions and fry 2-3 more minutes.

2. Add the remaining ingredients. Bring to a boil, simmer, covered, stirring occasionally, for 50 minutes, or until the beets are tender.

Creamy Artichoke Casserole

——◆——

Jerusalem artichokes are a nuisance to prepare because they are so knobby. This dish makes a very nice accompaniment to Braised Leeks with Zucchini or Fennel Bean Pot (see pages 95 and 102).

1 1/2 lbs Jerusalem artichokes,
  well scrubbed
2 onions
3 tablespoons low-fat soft cheese

salt and freshly ground black pepper
4 tablespoons whole-grain
  breadcrumbs

1. Steam the artichokes and onions in a steamer for about 35-40 minutes, or until the artichokes are soft. You can also boil them both in a little water for about 20-25 minutes. Drain, and peel the artichokes.

2. Preheat the oven to 375°F.

3. Mash the onions and artichokes together. Stir in the soft cheese and season with salt and pepper.

4. Spoon into a casserole dish, sprinkle with breadcrumbs, and bake for 30 minutes.

Artichokes Jerusalem

—◆—

1 large onion, chopped
2 tablespoons olive oil
1 1/2 lbs large Jerusalem artichokes
4 tomatoes, peeled (see page xi)
  and chopped
1 tablespoon tomato purée

1/2 teaspoon dried dill
salt and freshly ground black pepper
juice of 1 lemon
2 tablespoons chopped fresh parsley
1/2 cup water

1. In a large saucepan, fry the onion in the oil until well browned.

2. Meanwhile, wash and peel the artichokes and wash again. Cut into quarters and add to the onion. Toss well so that the artichoke quarters are coated in oil.

3. Add the remaining ingredients, stir, and bring to a boil. Cover and simmer, stirring occasionally, for 30-35 minutes, or until the artichokes are just tender the sauce is thick.

Celery with Provence Herbs

—◆—

I discovered this dish in a restaurant just under the walls of the Roman amphitheater in Orange. It uses classic Provence herbs which include fennel seeds—the secret here. It's equally good served hot or cold. For the cold version, simply add a tablespoon of lemon juice or cider vinegar.

1 head of celery, sliced
1 onion, finely sliced
1 tablespoon vegetable oil
1 tomato, peeled (see page xi),
  seeded, and chopped (optional)
1 tablespoon tomato purée
1/4 teaspoon fennel seeds

2 fresh rosemary sprigs or
  1/4 teaspoon dried rosemary
2 fresh thyme sprigs or
  1/4 teaspoon dried thyme
salt and freshly ground black pepper
1 tablespoon lemon juice or cider
  vinegar (if serving cold)

1. Steam the celery in a steamer for about 20-30 minutes, or until tender. You can also cook it in a little salted boiling water for 20-30 minutes, depending on the size and age of the celery.

2. Meanwhile, in a large saucepan fry the onion in the oil until it turns transparent. Add the tomato and tomato purée and all the herbs and spices. Simmer for about 8-10 minutes, adding a little water if the mixture is too dry.

3. When the celery is cooked, drain well, and mix with the tomato sauce. Serve hot or let cool and add a tablespoon of lemon juice or cider vinegar.

Celery Root and Tomato Casserole

—◆—

Celery root tends to be an underrated vegetable, but it has a lovely flavor reminiscent of celery and parsnips. Take care when preparing it, as it discolors quickly. Rub cut surfaces with lemon or drop into water with a little lemon juice or vinegar added to it.

1 onion, sliced
1 tablespoon vegetable oil
1 medium celery root, diced
1 14-oz can of tomatoes

1/4 teaspoon grated lemon rind
juice of 1/2 lemon
pinch of mixed herbs
salt and freshly ground black pepper

1. In a large saucepan fry the onion in the oil for about 3-4 minutes, or until it turns transparent.

2. Add the celery root and continue to fry for 2-3 more minutes.

3. Add the remaining ingredients and bring to a boil. Simmer for 40 minutes, or until the celery root is tender and the sauce is fairly thick.

Lettuce with Scallions and Peas

—◆—

This is a good dish to make with the very first fresh peas. The other ingredients help to make a few peas go a lot further.

1 medium head of crisp lettuce
1 bunch scallions
3/4 cup peas
2 tablespoons butter

1/2-1 teaspoon sugar
3 tablespoons water
2 parsley sprigs

1. Cut the lettuce into quarters, wash, and drain well.

2. Place all the ingredients in a large saucepan and bring to a boil. Cover and reduce the heat. Simmer for about 20 minutes, or until all the vegetables are tender.

3. Transfer to a warmed serving dish. Remove the parsley and serve.

Persian-Style Okra

—◆—

Okra is one of the basic vegetables of Iran (formerly Persia) and is used in all kinds of dishes from soups to stews. This is good served with spicy dishes.

1 lb okra
1 large onion, sliced
1 garlic clove, chopped
1 tablespoon olive oil
4 tomatoes, peeled (see page xi)
  and chopped

1/2 teaspoon ground coriander
1/4 teaspoon ground turmeric
salt and freshly ground black pepper
juice of 1/2 lemon

1. Cut the stems off the okra, being careful not to cut into the main body of the vegetable.

2. In a large saucepan, fry the onion and garlic in the oil until very lightly browned. Add the okra and fry for 1-2 minutes.

3. Add the remaining ingredients. Bring to a boil, cover, and simmer for about 20-30 minutes, or until the okra is tender. Do not overcook the okra or it will be mushy and slimy.

Zucchini Hongroise

—◆—

One of my favorite Hungarian restaurants in London serves zucchini this way and, after some persuasion, the chef finally consented to part with the recipe.

1 small onion, sliced
1 teaspoon butter
1 lb zucchini, cut into small cubes
2 tablespoons chopped fresh dill
  or 1 tablespoon dried dill

1 large pickled cucumber, sliced
1 tablespoon vegetable stock
  (see page x) or water
6 tablespoons whipping cream

1. Preheat the oven to 375°F.

2. In a pan, fry the onion in the butter until lightly browned. Set aside.

3. Place the zucchini in a casserole dish. Add the onion, dill, pickled cucumber, and stock or water. Cover and bake for 45 minutes.

4. Drain off the cooking liquid and mix it with the cream. Pour into a saucepan and bring it to a boil. Continue boiling for 3-4 minutes, then when the mixture thickens, pour it over the zucchini and serve.

Braised Leeks with Zucchini

—◆—

Baked leeks retain their flavor much better than steamed or boiled leeks. Serve with Savory Baked Rice or Potato and Mushroom Celeste (see pages 57 and 106).

1 tablespoon olive oil
6 large leeks
1 onion, sliced
1 tablespoon tomato purée

4 tablespoons water
salt and freshly ground black pepper
1/2 lb zucchini, sliced

1. Preheat the oven to 375°F.

2. Heat the oil in a frying pan until very hot. Cut the leeks coarsely and toss into the pan. Quickly brown and transfer them to a small casserole dish. Fry the onion and add it to the leeks.

3. Mix together the tomato purée and water and pour over the vegetables. Season with salt and pepper. Cover and bake for 30 minutes.

4. Add the zucchini, and continue baking for 15 more minutes.

Vegetarian Chili

—◆—

This delicious alternative to the original Tex-Mex dish gains in complementary protein if served with a rice dish. It goes well with a mixture of vegetarian Indian dishes, such as Aloo Gobi (see page 101), curried okra or eggplant, rice, and Raita (see page 169).

1 onion, finely chopped
1 garlic clove, finely chopped
3 tablespoons vegetable oil
1/2 lb mushrooms, finely chopped
1 medium eggplant, finely diced
2 tablespoons tomato purée
1/2 cup red or white wine

3-4 tablespoons water or vegetable
 stock (see page x)
1-2 teaspoons chili powder to taste
1/2 teaspoon ground cumin
pinch of mixed herbs
1 10-oz can of red kidney beans,
 drained

1. In a large saucepan, fry the onion and garlic in the oil until lightly browned or softened. Add the mushrooms and continue cooking for 3-4 minutes, stirring constantly.

2. Add the remaining ingredients except the beans and bring to a boil. Reduce the heat and simmer for 30 minutes.

3. Stir in the beans and cook 10 more minutes.

Malaysian Vegetable-Fruit Curry

—◆—

Tamarind and lemongrass contribute a lovely lemony flavor in this mild curry from Southeast Asia. In a pinch you could use one or the other or, if you cannot find them at all, substitute lemon juice. The flavor will not be quite the same, but it will still be very good.

1 tablespoon freshly grated ginger
2 garlic cloves, crushed
2 pieces lemongrass
1 onion, sliced
1 tablespoon vegetable oil
1 tablespoon tamarind paste,
   seeds removed
1 tablespoon curry powder

1-1 1/2 cups vegetable stock
   (see page x)
1 1/2 pounds mixed vegetables
   (carrots, potatoes, green beans,
   radish, peas, cauliflower)
2 tablespoons raisins
1 8-oz can of pineapple chunks,
   drained

1. In a large saucepan, fry the ginger, garlic, lemongrass, and onion in the oil for 2-3 minutes. Stir in the tamarind paste, curry powder, and stock, and bring to a boil.

2. Add all the vegetables except the cauliflower. Simmer for 35-45 minutes.

3. Add the cauliflower, raisins, and pineapple. Simmer for 10 more minutes.

Tarka Dhal

This punchy version of Indian lentil *dhal* goes with any curry. It is also very good cooked a little longer and served in taco shells with shredded lettuce and grated cheese.

1/2 cup lentils
2 cups water
1 teaspoon turmeric
pinch of salt

1 small onion, sliced
2 garlic cloves, crushed
2 tablespoons grated fresh ginger
1 tablespoon vegetable oil

1. Place the lentils in a pan with the water, bring to a boil, and simmer for 45 minutes.

2. Add the turmeric and salt and continue cooking about 30 minutes, or until the lentils are really soft.

3. In a frying pan, fry the onion, garlic, and ginger in the oil until well browned. Add to the lentils just before serving.

Tortino di Zucchini

——◆——

I owe a debt of thanks to Anna del Conte for the idea for this Italian-based dish of zucchini and tomatoes. Chopped nuts can be used instead of cheese.

1 1/2 lbs zucchini, thickly sliced
salt
2 small onions, sliced
3 garlic cloves, chopped
2 tablespoons olive oil
1 15-oz can of tomatoes,
  coarsely chopped or puréed

2 tablespoons chopped fresh parsley
fresh basil leaves
freshly ground black pepper
2 slices of rye bread, made into
  breadcrumbs
2 oz Romano cheese

1. Place the zucchini in a colander over a plate. Sprinkle generously with salt and let stand.

2. In a large saucepan, fry the onions and garlic in the oil until softened and lightly browned. Add the tomatoes, parsley, basil, and pepper and bring to a boil. Simmer for 15-20 minutes until fairly thick.

3. Preheat the oven to 400°F.

4. Wash the salted zucchini well, drain, and pat dry. Add to the tomato sauce and cook for about 10 minutes until *al dente*. Transfer to a baking dish.

5. Mix the breadcrumbs and cheese and sprinkle over the zucchini and sauce. Place in the oven and bake for 15-20 minutes. Let stand for 4-5 minutes before serving.

Butterbean Country Casserole

——◆——

This substantial dish is almost a full meal in itself. All it needs is a bowl of salad and some fruit.

4 small onions, sliced
3 tablespoons vegetable oil
3/4 lb mushrooms, sliced
2 15-oz cans of butterbeans, drained

6-8 tomatoes, chopped
salt and freshly ground black pepper
4 oz cheddar cheese, grated
1/2 cup breadcrumbs

1. In a saucepan, fry the onions in the oil until transparent. Add the sliced mushrooms and continue frying for 5-6 minutes.

2. Add the beans and tomatoes and season with salt and pepper. Heat through.

3. Place in a baking dish and sprinkle with the cheese and breadcrumbs. Brown under the broiler and serve at once.

African Curried Vegetables

———◆———

Peanuts, or groundnuts as they are sometimes called, crop up in all kinds of African dishes. Here peanut butter gives a lovely smoothness to the sauce.

1 onion, chopped
2 garlic cloves, crushed
2 teaspoons freshly grated ginger
2 tablespoons vegetable oil
4 cardamom pods, slightly crushed
2 cloves
1 tablespoon ground coriander

1 teaspoon ground cumin
1 lb mixed vegetables (cauliflower,
 carrots, potatoes)
2 cups water
1 heaping tablespoon peanut butter
salt and freshly ground black pepper

1. In a large saucepan, fry the onion, garlic, and ginger in the oil. Add the cardamom, cloves, coriander, and cumin and continue cooking for 2-3 minutes.

2. Add the chopped vegetables and water. Bring to a boil, cover, and simmer for about 30-40 minutes.

3. Drain off the liquid and mix with the peanut butter. Return it to the pan and season with salt and pepper. Simmer for 5-10 more minutes before serving.

Mixed Vegetables
with Sunflower Seed Dumplings

—◆—

This recipe from the American Midwest is a dumpling lover's dream. The sunflower seeds give a nutty texture to the dumplings and the tabasco adds a zing to the vegetables.

2 tablespoons vegetable oil
2 leeks, sliced
1 large red pepper, seeded and
 cut into 1/2-inch squares
2 tablespoons flour
1 14-oz can of tomatoes
1/2 cup vegetable stock (see page x)
1 lb rutabaga, cut into large dice
1/2 lb parsnips, cut into large dice
dash of tabasco

Dumplings
1/3 cup margarine
3/4 cup whole-wheat self-rising flour
4 tablespoons sunflower seeds
cold water

1/2 lb zucchini, thickly sliced
3/4 lb mushrooms, wiped and thickly
 sliced
salt and freshly ground black pepper

1. Heat the oil in a large saucepan and simmer the leeks and pepper for 3 minutes. Stir in the flour and cook for 1 minute. Gradually stir in the tomatoes and stock. Bring to a boil, stirring constantly.

2. Add the rutabaga, parsnips, and tabasco. Cover and simmer for 15 minutes, stirring occasionally.

3. Meanwhile, make the dumplings. Rub the margarine into the flour and stir in the sunflower seeds. Add just enough cold water to form a not-too-stiff dough. Shape into 12 balls.

4. Stir the zucchini and mushrooms into the simmered vegetables and season with salt and pepper. Top with the dumplings. Cover and simmer 20 minutes.

Aloo Gobi

— ◆ —

I serve this cauliflower and potato curry with Tarka Dhal (see page 97), rice, and lots of papadums. The best way to cook the latter is in the microwave. They take about 1 minute on full power and come out crisp and not at all fatty.

1 tablespoon vegetable oil
1/4 teaspoon coriander seeds
1/8 teaspoon cumin seeds
2-3 cloves
2 small cauliflowers or
  1/2 medium cauliflower, broken
  into florets
3/4 lb potatoes, peeled and cut into
  large dice

1 teaspoon each of ground cumin
  and ground coriander
1/2 teaspoon ground turmeric
1 small green chile, seeded and
  finely chopped (optional)
salt and freshly ground black pepper
1/2 cup yogurt

1. Heat the oil in a small heavy pan and fry the coriander seeds, cumin seeds, and cloves over high heat about 1/2-3/4 minute, or until they begin to pop.

2. Add the remaining ingredients and bring to a boil. Cover and simmer for 15-20 minutes, or until the vegetables are tender and the juices are fairly thick and creamy.

Fennel Bean Pot

—◆—

Fennel seeds are worth seeking out for this unusual bean pot. It is also worth the trouble of using dried rather than canned beans. The longer cooking time allows all the flavors to meld.

1/4 lb dried Great Northern beans
1/4 lb dried black-eyed peas
1/4 lb dried butterbeans
2 onions, chopped
2 garlic cloves, chopped
1 tablespoon vegetable oil

1/2 teaspoon whole fennel seeds
2 tablespoons fresh chopped chervil
*   or parsley*
salt and freshly ground black pepper
1 cup red wine

1. Soak the beans and peas in cold water overnight.

2. Preheat the oven to 375°F.

3. In a saucepan, fry the onions and garlic in the oil until golden. Add the beans and peas along with the fennel seeds and chervil, and season with salt and pepper.

4. Transfer to an earthenware casserole dish and add in the red wine. Cover and bake for 1 1/2 hours.

5. Increase the temperature to 400°F and bake for 40-45 more minutes, stirring occasionally.

EGG AND CHEESE DISHES

—◆—

These dishes have eggs and/or cheese as their major ingredient. They should be served with one or two vegetable dishes, or perhaps a salad and potatoes. Marinated Brie can be served as a starter or even a final course, or with a large main-course salad. Smaller versions of Cheese Nut Patties are a welcome part of a canapé buffet, and Individual Sun-Dried Tomato Quiches and Pepper and Olive Tartlets can also be served on a hot or cold buffet.

Marinated Brie

—◆—

Any soft cheese with a rind works well in this recipe. The cheese seems to take up the flavors, particularly of the oil (which must be extra-virgin, the best grade of olive oil).

1/2 cup extra-virgin olive oil
12 black peppercorns
2 garlic cloves, chopped

1 teaspoon dried mixed herbs
3/4 lb Brie, cut into slices
pinch of salt

1. Heat the oil in a small pan with the peppercorns, garlic, and herbs. When the mixture starts to bubble, remove from the heat and let cool.

2. Arrange the slices of Brie in a shallow dish. Add the salt to the cooked oil and spoon over the cheese. Let stand for at least 4 hours before serving.

Gratin of Kohlrabi

—◆—

Though less well known here, kohlrabi has been a favorite vegetable in Germany. This dish makes a rich but unusual starter, or it may be served as a vegetable accompaniment to a casserole.

4 kohlrabi, peeled and sliced
salt

1/2 cup whipping cream
2 egg yolks

1. Cook the kohlrabi in very little salted boiling water until just tender. Drain, retaining the cooking liquid. Place the kohlrabi slices in 4 individual baking dishes and keep warm.

2. Bring the cooking liquid to a boil again and continue boiling until it is reduced to about 3 tablespoons.

3. Lightly whisk the cream with the egg yolks. Pour this mixture into the vegetable liquid and simmer, whisking constantly. Do not allow the mixture to boil. When the mixture begins to thicken a little, pour it over the kohlrabi.

4. Place the dishes under a hot broiler until a thin golden skin forms on the surface. Serve at once.

Celery Cheese Gratin

—◆—

Serve this unusual celery dish—which has a light but crunchy texture—for lunch or dinner, with potatoes and another vegetable.

1 small head of celery
2 tablespoons milk
1/2 lb cheddar cheese, grated
2 eggs, beaten

pinch of celery salt
freshly ground black pepper
4 tablespoons fresh whole-wheat
breadcrumbs

1. Preheat the oven to 350°F.

2. Grate the celery on a medium grater. Place in a saucepan with the milk. Bring to a boil and simmer, stirring occasionally, for about 15-20 minutes, or until the celery is tender. Let cool.

3. Mix the celery with the cheese, eggs, celery salt, and pepper. Spoon into a greased casserole dish, cover with breadcrumbs, and bake for 30-35 minutes.

Italian Potato and Romano Pie

—◆—

I serve this dish with a mass of grilled tomatoes topped with a little pesto sauce (see page 49).

2 lbs potatoes, peeled
1 bunch scallions, sliced
1 garlic clove, crushed
5 oz Romano cheese

4 eggs, beaten
1 cup yogurt
salt and freshly ground black pepper

1. Preheat the oven to 400°F.

2. Grate the potatoes on a medium grater into a colander and squeeze thoroughly with a paper towel to remove all the water.

3. Mix with the remaining ingredients and spoon into a greased shallow baking dish. Bake for 1 hour, or until crispy on top.

Cheese Nut Patties

—◆—

It's worth cooking the potatoes from scratch for these flavorful and interestingly textured patties. Tofu can be used in place of cottage cheese.

MAKES 8

1 1/2 lbs potatoes
salt
1 1/2 cups cottage cheese
1/2 cup ground roasted peanuts
2 tablespoons chopped fresh chives
  or scallions

salt and freshly ground black pepper
4 tablespoons fresh breadcrumbs,
  toasted
vegetable oil to shallow-fry

1. Cook the potatoes in boiling salted water until tender, then peel. Mash with the cottage cheese and peanuts.

2. Add the chives or scallions and season with salt and pepper. Mix well.

3. Divide the mixture into 8 portions and shape into balls. Roll in breadcrumbs until coated all over and flatten into patties.

4. In a frying pan, shallow-fry in the oil on both sides until golden, about 4-5 minutes.

Potato and Mushroom Celeste

—◆—

Instead of Brie I sometimes use Camembert in this dish for a stronger flavor. Be careful if you do, since the taste can be a bit overwhelming if the cheese is too ripe.

1 1/2 lbs potatoes, peeled and sliced
3 onions, sliced
4 tomatoes, peeled (see page xi)
  and sliced
1/2 lb mushrooms, sliced

1/2 lb Brie cheese, sliced
1 teaspoon dried summer savory
1/2 teaspoon garlic salt
salt and freshly ground black pepper
1/2 cup whipping cream

1. Preheat the oven to 400°F.

2. Layer the vegetables and cheese in a casserole dish, sprinkling each layer with savory, garlic salt, salt, and pepper. Finish with a layer of potatoes.

3. Pour the cream over the top, cover, and bake for about 45 minutes.

Individual Sun-Dried Tomato Quiches

These quiches are so good that I make six and serve four as a main course and use the remaining two for packed lunches the next day. I use half-quantity of the pastry recipe given on page 148 for Pâtés de Béziers, but you can use any kind of pastry, including ready-made or frozen ones.

Makes 6

1/2 lb pastry
2 tablespoons sun-dried tomatoes
2 eggs, beaten

4 tablespoons grated Parmesan cheese
4 tablespoons yogurt
salt and freshly ground black pepper

1. Preheat the oven to 375°F.

2. Roll out the pastry and use to line six 4-inch tartlet tins. Chill these until you are ready.

3. Pour sufficient boiling water over the tomatoes just to cover them and let them stand for 15 minutes. Drain and slice thinly.

4. Mix the eggs with the cheese and yogurt, stir in the tomato strips, and season with salt and pepper. Spoon into the pastry-lined tins and bake for 25-30 minutes.

Pepper and Olive Tartlets

—◆—

This variation on the quiche theme uses cottage cheese. Silken tofu can be substituted. Red peppers give the sweetest flavor but green ones can also be used.

MAKES 6

1/2 lb pastry
1 lb red peppers, seeded and
  quartered
1 egg

1/4 lb cottage cheese
salt and freshly ground black pepper
12 black olives, pitted

1. Preheat the oven to 375°F.

2. Roll out the pastry and use to line six 4-inch tartlet tins.

3. Place the pieces of pepper skin side up on a broiler tray and broil under high heat until lightly seared all over. Remove to a bowl and cover with a lid. Let stand for 10-15 minutes, then peel and discard the skin. Cut into strips.

4. Beat the egg with the cottage cheese and stir in the peppers. Season with salt and pepper. Spoon into the pastry-lined tins, dot with olives, and bake for 35 minutes. Serve warm or cold.

Cauliflower Soufflé

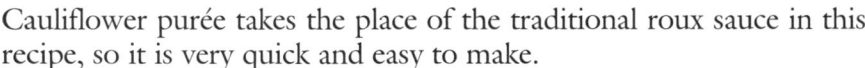

Cauliflower purée takes the place of the traditional roux sauce in this recipe, so it is very quick and easy to make.

1 medium cauliflower
3 eggs, separated

salt and freshly ground black pepper

1. Preheat the oven to 400°F and grease 4 individual soufflé dishes.

2. Steam the cauliflower until soft, then rub through a sieve or process it until smooth. Let cool.

3. Mix the egg yolks with the cauliflower purée and season with salt and pepper.

4. Whisk the egg whites until stiff, then fold into the cauliflower mixture.

5. Pour into 4 individual soufflé dishes and bake for 10-15 minutes, or until set and slightly brown on top.

Chive and Tomato Soufflé

——◆——

Tomatoes and chives are a winning combination whatever time of the year, but the flavors always remind me of summer. To make individual soufflés, divide the mixture among six to eight ramekins (depending on size) and bake for 20 minutes.

1 cup milk
1 tablespoon tomato purée
1/3 cup butter
1/4 cup flour
4 whole eggs, separated, plus
  1 extra egg white

2 oz hard cheese, grated
1 bunch of fresh chives, chopped
1/2 cup peeled (see page xi) and
  chopped tomatoes

1. Preheat the oven to 375°F.

2. In a bowl, mix together the milk and tomato purée. Melt the butter in a saucepan. Add the flour and cook for 1 minute.

3. Gradually add the milk and tomato mixture and bring to a boil, stirring constantly. Cook for 3 minutes.

4. Remove from the heat and beat in the egg yolks, then stir in the cheese, chives, and tomatoes.

5. Whisk the egg whites until stiff, then stir a couple of tablespoons into the soufflé mixture. Fold in the rest of the egg whites, then spoon into a greased soufflé dish.

6. Bake for 45-50 minutes, or until golden brown and set in the center. Serve at once.

South American Baked Eggs

——◆——

This variation on eggs in potato nests has lots of flavor and makes a good snack or light dinner dish. Serve with a tossed green salad and crusty rolls.

4 onions, chopped
1 green pepper, seeded and chopped
2 tablespoons vegetable oil
1 14-oz can of red kidney beans, drained

1 teaspoon dried thyme
salt and freshly ground black pepper
4 large eggs
4 tablespoons red wine

1. Preheat the oven to 425°F.

2. In a pan, fry the onions and pepper in the oil until softened.

3. Mash the beans with a fork and add to the onions and pepper with the thyme. Season with salt and pepper. Mix well and spoon into a baking dish.

4. Make 4 wells in the mixture and break an egg into each one. Pour the wine over the top and bake for about 15-20 minutes, or until the eggs are set.

Grated Vegetable Rosti

——◆——

There is no need to precook the potatoes for this variation on the Swiss specialty. Different vegetables, such as grated celery root or parsnips, can be added to the potato base in place of carrots and celery. Serve with spinach or beans to make a satisfying meal.

1 large carrot, grated
3 celery stalks, sliced very thinly
1 onion, grated
2 large potatoes, peeled

3 large eggs, beaten
salt and freshly ground black pepper
2 tablespoons vegetable oil

1. Place the grated vegetables in a colander, making sure to grate the potatoes last since they tend to discolor. Squeeze out all the water by pressing with paper towels. Mix the vegetables with the eggs and season with salt and pepper.

2. Heat the oil in a frying pan and spoon the vegetable mixture into it. Spread out to cover the base of the pan and turn the heat down. Cook slowly for about 15-20 minutes, or until well browned underneath. Turn the mixture over with a spatula and cook on the other side for 10-15 more minutes.

Polenta-Stuffed Peppers

Popular in Italy, polenta or yellow cornmeal is used to make dumplings or is served as an accompaniment to other dishes. My Romanian friend uses it to stuff multi-colored peppers in this recipe.

4 medium peppers of different colors
2 cups water
1 teaspoon salt
1/2 cup polenta
2 tablespoons butter

3 oz Parmesan or
*   any hard cheese, grated*
freshly ground black pepper
3 eggs

1. Preheat the oven to 350°F.

2. Cut the stalk ends off the peppers and scoop out the center membranes and seeds. Place them on a baking dish and bake for 10 minutes. Remove from the oven.

3. Meanwhile, pour the water, salt, and polenta into a heavy-bottomed pan. Slowly bring to a boil, stirring constantly. Reduce the heat and simmer, stirring frequently, for about 15-20 minutes, or until the polenta is fairly thick.

4. Remove from the heat and beat in the butter, cheese, pepper, and eggs, one at a time.

5. Spoon this mixture into the hot peppers and bake for 40 minutes.

Fava Bean and Herb Omelette

—◆—

Fava beans seem to go very well with eggs, and here they are used to fill an omelette. This recipe is sufficient for two people, so double it for four.

MAKES 6

1/2 cup shelled fava beans
salt
2 tablespoons chopped fresh parsley
2 teaspoons chopped fresh chives
1 teaspoon chopped fresh summer
  savory or oregano

4 eggs
2 tablespoons water
salt and freshly ground black pepper
pat of butter

1. Cook the beans in lightly salted boiling water for about 10-15 minutes, or until tender. Drain well, and mix with the herbs.

2. Beat the eggs, water, salt, and pepper together with a fork. Melt the butter in an omelette pan and when hot pour in the egg mixture. Stir lightly 2-3 times only. Cook until just set.

3. Place the bean and herb mixture over one half of the omelette and fold the other half over it.

Vietnamese Egg Pancakes

—◆—

I first had these spicy filled pancakes in a Vietnamese restaurant in the south of France. They fall somewhere between a flat omelette and a crispy pancake. This quantity makes quite a filling main course.

Pancakes
2 cups boiling water
1 cup coconut flakes
1 small onion, thinly sliced
2 tablespoons vegetable oil
pinch of whole cumin seeds
1/3 cup rice or potato flour
2 tablespoons whole-wheat flour, sieved
1/4 teaspoon ground turmeric
3 large eggs, beaten

Filling
1 large garlic clove, crushed
1 tablespoon freshly grated ginger
6 scallions, sliced lengthwise
3-4 tablespoons olive oil
1/3 lb button mushrooms, thickly sliced
1/2 lb zucchini, cut into strips
1/2 lb bean sprouts
1 tablespoon soy sauce (optional)

1. To make the pancakes, pour the boiling water over the coconut. Let stand for about 20-30 minutes. Squeeze out the liquid from the coconut to make 1 cup coconut milk.

2. In a pan, fry the onion with the cumin seeds in 1 tablespoon of the oil until well browned.

3. Mix the two flours with the turmeric, then stir in the eggs, coconut milk, and fried onion and cumin seeds.

4. Heat the remaining oil in a 12-inch nonstick frying pan, and spoon a quarter of the pancake mixture into the pan. Tilt and roll the pan until the mixture is spread out well. Cook until well browned and slightly crisp underneath, then turn over and cook the other side until also brown and slightly crisp. Remove and keep warm. Make 3 more pancakes in the same way and keep warm.

5. To make the filling, stir-fry the garlic, ginger, and scallions in the oil. Add the mushrooms and stir-fry for another minute, then add the zucchini, bean sprouts, and soy sauce. Fry for another 2 minutes.

6. Spoon onto the pancakes and fold over. Serve at once.

SALADS

———◆———

These salads are varied and very versatile. They can be served as a first course or as an accompaniment to the main course. Some, like Chicory Salad and Fresh Lentil and Radish Salad, make main-course dishes in their own right. Most salads benefit from a good dressing, which may be based on oil and vinegar, oil and lemon juice, yogurt, tofu, or cheese. I personally think the best oil to use for salads is olive oil. If you're not sure about the flavor, try a plain olive oil first, and then move on to the more fully flavored virgin and extra-virgin oils.

Tofu Dressing for Mixed Green Salad

———◆———

This easy-to-make dressing can be flavored in lots of different ways. Simply add your chosen flavoring to the mixture in the blender. You may need to add a little water if using fresh tofu. This dressing can be stored in the refrigerator for two to three days.

1/3 lb tofu
2 tablespoons lemon juice or wine
  vinegar

2 tablespoons olive oil
salt and freshly ground black pepper

1. Purée all the ingredients in a blender or food processor, or mash with a fork and mix with a wire whisk. Stir in your chosen flavorings.

Suggested flavorings

3 tablespoons each chopped scallions and parsley

or

1 teaspoon curry powder mixed with 1 tablespoon mild chutney

or

1 tablespoon peanut butter or tahini paste

Sala Beet Salad

———◆———

This mixture, derived from a more elaborate salad I encountered when staying with a family in Finland, makes an excellent side salad for a lasagne, Pasticcio (see page 53), and other pasta dishes.

1/2 lb cooked beets, peeled and diced
1 large pickled cucumber, diced
1 teaspoon grated orange rind
1/2 bunch watercress

Dressing
2 tablespoons olive oil
freshly ground black pepper

1. Toss together in a bowl the beets, pickled cucumber, and orange rind, then spoon onto a bed of watercress arranged on a serving plate.

2. Just before serving, drizzle the oil over the salad and sprinkle with pepper.

Cauliflower Salad

———◆———

Cauliflower is very good eaten raw. Try small florets as dippers for guacamole (see page 161) or use them in this crunchy winter salad.

1/2 cauliflower, cut into small florets
1 green apple, cored and diced
1 7-oz can of red pimentos, drained
  and finely chopped
1 cucumber, diced

1 tablespoon slivered almonds

Dressing
3 tablespoons olive oil
1 tablespoon white wine vinegar

1. Place all the salad ingredients in a bowl and toss lightly together.

2. Mix the oil and vinegar in another bowl and pour over the top of the salad. Chill for half an hour. Toss again and serve.

Eggplant Salad

———◆———

This recipe originates in the Middle East, where it is usually served with hot pita bread.

2 eggplants
1/2 green pepper, seeded
  and finely chopped
2 tomatoes, peeled (see page xi),
  seeded, and chopped
1/2 small onion, finely chopped

1 garlic clove, crushed
1 teaspoon ground cumin
1 tablespoon chopped fresh parsley
2 teaspoons olive oil
juice of 1 lemon
salt and freshly ground black pepper

1. Preheat the oven to 400°F.

2. Bake the eggplants in their skins about 1 hour, or until the skins blacken and they feel soft to the touch. Let cool.

3. Cut open the eggplants and scrape out all the flesh. Discard the skin and finely chop the flesh into a bowl. Mix with the remaining ingredients and season with salt and pepper. Serve garnished with a little more parsley.

Carrot and Fennel Coleslaw

———◆———

Cabbage is, of course, the usual base for coleslaw, but there is no reason why other vegetables should not be used in the same way.

3 carrots, cut into long thin sticks
1 head of fennel, finely sliced
3 tablespoons mayonnaise

1/2 teaspoon Dijon mustard
freshly ground black pepper

1. Blanch the carrots and fennel for 3 minutes in boiling water, then plunge into cold water for the same amount of time. Drain well.

2. Mix the mayonnaise with the mustard and pepper in a bowl and toss with the completely cooled vegetables. Store in the refrigerator until required.

Broccoli Salad

———◆———

Take care not to overcook the broccoli for this salad. If you do, it will be mushy and unpleasant. The dressing is quite substantial and full of flavor.

1 lb broccoli
salt

Dressing
1 hard-boiled egg, chopped
1 tomato, peeled (see page xi),
* seeded, and chopped*
1 small pickled cucumber,
* finely chopped*

4 scallions, finely chopped
6 tablespoons olive oil
2 tablespoons cider or white wine
* vinegar*
freshly ground black pepper
1 teaspoon chopped fresh tarragon
* or 1/4 teaspoon dried tarragon*

1. Steam the broccoli or cook it in a little salted boiling water. Drain and let cool.

2. Mix the egg, tomato, pickled cucumber, and scallions in a small bowl.

3. In another bowl, mix the oil with the remaining ingredients and beat well, then mix with the egg-tomato mixture. Chill in the refrigerator.

4. Arrange the pieces of broccoli on 4 small serving plates. Pour the dressing over the top and serve.

Marinated Mushroom and Avocado Salad

—◆—

A ripe avocado will yield slightly to gentle pressure. Unripe avocados will ripen in the fruit bowl in a couple of days. Choose only really ripe avocados for this salad and mix in at the last minute. Serve on a bed of mixed salad leaves or with Chinese bean sprouts.

1/2 lb small button mushrooms, quartered
1/3 cup olive oil
2 tablespoons fresh lemon juice
1 teaspoon tomato purée
1/4 teaspoon dried thyme
pinch of fennel seeds
salt and freshly ground black pepper

1/4 lb cashew nuts
1/4 green pepper, seeded and finely chopped
2 scallions, finely chopped
pinch of grated lemon rind
1 large or 2 small avocados, chopped
parsley sprigs

1. Mix in a bowl the mushrooms, oil, lemon juice, tomato purée, thyme, and fennel. Season with salt and pepper. Let stand for at least 1 hour, stirring occasionally.

2. Meanwhile, dry-fry the cashew nuts in a hot frying pan, being sure not to burn them. Cool.

3. Just before serving, add the cashew nuts to the mushroom mixture plus the remaining ingredients except the parsley. Toss well together and serve garnished with parsley.

Cauliflower and Grilled Red Pepper Salad

—◆—

This can be served very successfully either as part of a cold buffet or as a first course. The idea comes from Italy, where they favor capers in their cooking.

SERVES 8-10

1 cauliflower

4 red peppers, seeded and cut into quarters

8 fresh tarragon sprigs, divided

Dressing

6 tablespoons extra-virgin olive oil

1 tablespoon red wine vinegar

salt and freshly ground black pepper

1/4 garlic clove, crushed

8 fresh parsley sprigs

40 black olives, pitted and quartered

3 tablespoons capers, dried

1. Steam the cauliflower for 4-5 minutes. Cover and let cool, then break into florets.

2. Grill the peppers skin side up until the skins blacken. Place in a bowl, cover with a plate, and let cool. Peel off and discard the skin, then cut the flesh into strips.

3. Chop 1 large sprig of the tarragon and mix it with all the dressing ingredients in another bowl. Set aside.

4. Arrange the parsley on a serving plate and place strips of peppers on top. Dot with the cauliflower and sprinkle with olives and capers. Spoon the dressing over the top and add the remaining sprigs of tarragon. Serve at once.

Mixed Leaf and Pistachio Nut Salad

——◆——

Toasting nuts under the broiler or in a hot frying pan adds an extra dimension to their flavor, but be careful not to burn them.

5-6 pieces of sun-dried tomatoes
1 bunch watercress
mixed salad leaves
3 tablespoons shelled pistachio nuts,
* toasted (see page xi)*
3 tablespoons pine nuts, toasted
* (see page xi)*
8 baby artichoke hearts in oil
* (optional)*

16 black olives, pitted and halved
fresh herb sprigs

Dressing
6 tablespoons extra-virgin olive oil
1 tablespoon orange or tarragon
* vinegar*
salt and freshly ground black pepper

1. Soak the tomatoes in boiling water for 15-20 minutes. Drain and cut into strips.

2. Mix the watercress and salad leaves and strew them over 4 plates. Sprinkle with pistachio nuts, pine nuts, and the tomato strips. Dot with artichokes, if desired, olives, and sprigs of herbs.

3. Combine the dressing ingredients in a bowl, then pour over the salad just before serving.

Bitter Salad with Grilled Red Peppers

——◆——

Choose two or three different types of greens for this piquant Italian salad.

1 large or two small red peppers,
* seeded and quartered*
mixed bitter leaves (rocket, arugula,
* French dandelion, watercress,*
* sorrel)*
6-10 black olives, pitted and halved

1 teaspoon capers, drained

Dressing
6 tablespoons extra-virgin olive oil
1 tablespoon balsamic or sherry
* vinegar*
salt and freshly ground black pepper

1. Place the pepper pieces skin side up under a hot broiler until they begin to blacken. Place in a bowl and cover with a plate. Let cool. Remove and discard the skin and cut the flesh into strips.

2. Arrange the bitter leaves on 4 serving plates. Top with the pepper strips and sprinkle with the olives and capers.

3. Combine the dressing ingredients in a bowl, then pour over the salad just before serving.

Warm Bean Sprout Salad with Feta Cheese

— ◆ —

Warming the dressing brings out the full flavor of the olive oil, so choose a good one. Add the dressing at the last minute or the bean sprouts will lose their crunch.

6 oz Chinese bean sprouts
1/2 head of iceberg lettuce,
  shredded
12 small black olives, pitted and
  halved
2 tablespoons salted peanuts

Dressing
1 tablespoon olive oil
1 tablespoon lemon juice

4 oz feta cheese, crumbled
pinch of dried oregano
freshly ground black pepper

1. Toss together the bean sprouts and lettuce in a bowl. Sprinkle with olives and nuts.

2. To make the dressing, heat the oil and lemon juice in a saucepan. Pour over the top of the salad.

3. Sprinkle the salad with feta cheese, oregano, and pepper.

Arugula Salad with Chickpeas

—◆—

SERVES 2

3-4 sun-dried tomatoes

Dressing
4 tablespoons extra-virgin olive oil
2 teaspoons lemon juice
pinch of grated lemon rind
2 tablespoons chopped fresh parsley

2 teaspoons chopped fresh tarragon
salt and freshly ground black pepper

3/4 cup canned chickpeas, drained
fresh parsley and tarragon sprigs
1/2 cup packed arugula
fresh herb sprigs

1. Cover the tomatoes with boiling water and let stand for 15-20 minutes.

2. Mix all the dressing ingredients together in a bowl.

3. Place the chickpeas in another bowl and cover with the dressing.

4. Toss the parsley, tarragon, and arugula together, and arrange on 2 serving plates. Spoon the chickpeas and dressing over the top.

5. Drain the tomatoes and cut into strips. Arrange with sprigs of fresh herbs on the top of the salad and serve at once.

Chicory Salad

—◆—

I find that, with the eggs and cheese, this salad makes a real midday meal in itself. But if you think you will be hungry, add a home-made roll (see page 128).

1/2 cup frozen peas
salt
4 heads of chicory, sliced into circles
3 hard-boiled eggs, chopped
1/2 cup diced cheddar cheese
freshly ground black pepper

Dressing
2 tablespoons mayonnaise
1 teaspoon lemon juice
pinch of dried mixed herbs

watercress sprigs

1. Cook the peas in lightly salted boiling water for 2 minutes. Drain and rinse under the cold tap. Let cool in a sieve.

2. Mix in a bowl the chicory with the eggs, cheese, and cold peas, and season with pepper.

3. In another bowl, mix all the dressing ingredients together and add to the chicory mixture. Toss well and pile into the center of a serving dish. Surround with the sprigs of watercress.

Italian Panzanella Salad

——— ◆ ———

This bread-based salad comes from Tuscany, where the locals serve it any time of the day, from mid-morning to a late supper. Be sure to break the bread up into small pieces.

4 thick slices of Italian bread
4 tablespoons water
1 tablespoon red wine vinegar
2 large bunches basil,
  coarsely chopped

1 small bunch parsley,
  coarsely chopped
1 cucumber, diced
1 lb tomatoes, seeded and diced
6-8 tablespoons extra-virgin olive oil
basil sprigs

1. Place the slices of bread in a dish and pour the water and vinegar over them. Let stand for 30 minutes. Squeeze the bread dry, break it up with a fork, and put it into a bowl.

2. Add the remaining ingredients except the oil and basil. Toss well together.

3. Just before serving, add the oil and garnish with sprigs of basil. Serve at once.

French Lentil and Radish Salad

—◆—

The lentils can be cooked in advance and kept in the refrigerator until required. I like to cook double quantities of lentils and use half for this salad and the rest as extra garnish on other salads.

1 cup whole dried green or brown lentils
1 onion, stuck with 2 cloves
1 small carrot
1 bouquet garni
2 tablespoons olive oil
1 teaspoon cider vinegar
1 tablespoon chopped fresh parsley

1 teaspoon chopped fresh tarragon, chives, or dill
4 small scallions, finely chopped
salt and freshly ground black pepper
1 small cucumber, sliced
1/2 bunch radishes, sliced
1/2 green pepper, seeded and sliced
fresh herb (tarragon, chives, parsley) sprigs

1. Wash the lentils in cold water. Place in a saucepan with the onion, carrot, and *bouquet garni*. Cover with water and bring to a boil. Reduce the heat and simmer for 30 minutes, or until just tender. The lentils should retain their shape. Drain.

2. Mix in a bowl the lentils, oil, vinegar, fresh herbs, and scallions, and season with salt and pepper. Let cool.

3. Add the cucumber, radishes, and green pepper just before serving, and pile onto individual plates. Garnish with sprigs of fresh herbs.

SPECIAL OCCASION AND PARTY FOOD

DINNERS

If I am planning to entertain I am usually prepared to spend a little longer than usual in the kitchen. Accordingly, I have included some of my more elaborate favorites in this section.

However, I rarely prepare more than one complicated dish even when I am entertaining, and dishes like Vegetable Terrine or Baked Zucchini Molds would be followed by a quick-to-prepare pasta or stir-fry dish. Carrot Coulibiac, Red Pepper Gougère, Ratatouille Roulade, or Asparagus Pancake Stack might be preceded by a pre-prepared soup, interesting salad, or a quickly made hot starter such as Love Apples.

Complete the meal with a fresh fruit salad or an interesting cheese spread.

Whole-Wheat Rolls

This is my father's excellent recipe for crusty whole-wheat rolls.

MAKES 10-12

1 lb whole-wheat flour
1 tablespoon activated dried yeast

1 teaspoon salt
1 1/2 cups lukewarm water

1. Mix the flour, yeast, and salt in a large bowl. Make a well in the center and pour in the water. Mix to a soft, slightly sticky dough.

2. Turn onto a floured surface and knead for 10 minutes. Shape into rolls and place on a greased baking tray. Leave in a warm place about 1 hour, or until the rolls double their size.

3. Preheat the oven to 450°F.

4. Bake the rolls for 10-12 minutes. Tap the rolls with your fingernail—if they're done, they should sound hollow.

Herb and Lemon Bread

—◆—

This is a delicious variation on the popular garlic bread. It goes very well with delicately flavored salads, stir-fry dishes, or pasta.

SERVES 4-6

6 tablespoons butter, softened
2 tablespoons chopped fresh parsley
1 tablespoon chopped fresh chervil
1 tablespoon chopped fresh basil

fresh thyme leaves
1 teaspoon finely grated lemon rind
freshly ground black pepper
1 French baguette

1. Preheat the oven to 450°F.

2. In a bowl, mix the butter, herbs, lemon rind, and pepper to a soft paste.

3. Slice the baguette into thick chunks. Butter each slice with the herb mixture and press back into a loaf shape. Wrap in foil and bake for about 5-8 minutes, or until crisp. Serve at once.

Winter variation

If fresh herbs are not easily available, use 1/2 teaspoon mixed dried herbs, 1/2 teaspoon dried thyme, and 1/4 teaspoon dried rosemary.

Stuffed Pepper Rings

—◆—

You can vary the flavor of the stuffing by using different cheeses or by adding chopped herbs. Serve as a first course or on a cold buffet.

SERVES 6-8

4 green peppers
1/2 lb blue cheese, crumbled
3/4 lb cream cheese

1/2 cup grated cheddar cheese
4 tablespoons chopped walnuts
freshly ground black pepper

1. Cut the heads off the top of the peppers and scrape out the seeds and membranes.

2. Mix the remaining ingredients together in a bowl, then securely stuff the mixture into the hollow peppers. Place in a dish in the refrigerator and chill until the stuffing is firm.

3. To serve, cut the peppers horizontally into slices.

Venetian-Style Zucchini

—◆—

This unusual Italian dish makes a very good first course for dinner parties. Prepare all the ingredients and, as the guests sit down, begin to cook while your co-host serves the wine.

1 lb zucchini
2 tablespoons butter
1 tablespoon olive oil
1 egg

2 tablespoons grated Parmesan
cheese
1 tablespoon whipping cream
1 tablespoon chopped fresh parsley
salt and freshly ground black pepper

1. Slice the zucchini lengthwise. Cut each section into 2-3 thick sticks and then halve the sticks.

2. Heat the butter and oil in a frying pan and fry the zucchini over low heat for about 5 minutes. Do not let it brown.

3. Mix the remaining ingredients in a bowl, beat well, and pour into the pan. Stir everything with a wooden spoon, and as soon as the egg sets, serve with whole-wheat rolls (see page 128).

Carrot and Spinach Gâteau

——◆——

Cut this colorful savory gâteau just like a cake and serve in wedges. When I made this for a dinner party recently, I was unable to buy fresh spinach, so I substituted some Middle Eastern greens I found at the local Greek grocer. Frozen spinach doesn't work, however.

SERVES 6

1 lb carrots, sliced
6 tablespoons milk
2 tablespoons butter
8 eggs, beaten

1/4 teaspoon dried tarragon
salt and freshly ground black pepper
1/2 lb large spinach leaves, stalks
  removed

1. Preheat the oven to 375°F.

2. Cook the carrots in a little boiling water for about 10-12 minutes, or until tender. Drain well, and purée in a blender or food processor or mash well.

3. Heat the milk and butter in a pan. When the mixture boils, add the eggs and scramble until cooked. Add the tarragon and season with salt and pepper.

4. Blanch the spinach leaves by plunging them into boiling water for 1 minute, then refreshing them in cold water. Drain. Use all but one-fourth of the spinach to line a 6 1/2-inch spring-form pan.

5. Spoon half the egg mixture into the pan. Then add the carrot in one layer and top with the remaining egg. Cover with the remaining spinach. Cover with foil and bake for 30 minutes. Remove from the pan to serve.

Watercress Soufflé

—◆—

This makes an impressive first course. Soufflés are really not as difficult to prepare as many people think. The secret is to make sure that the soufflé is done so that it will not flop when you serve it.

2 bunches watercress
6 tablespoons butter
1/4 cup flour
1 cup milk

4 tablespoons grated cheddar cheese
1/2 teaspoon dry mustard
salt and freshly ground black pepper
4 eggs, separated

1. Preheat the oven to 375°F.

2. Blanch the watercress in boiling water for 3 minutes. Drain well and chop finely.

3. Melt the butter in a pan and stir in the flour. Gradually add the milk, stirring constantly. Bring to a boil and add the cheese, mustard, salt, pepper, and watercress. Cook for 3 minutes.

4. Remove from the heat and beat in the egg yolks.

5. In a bowl, whisk the egg whites until stiff. Mix 1 tablespoon of the whites into the soufflé mixture and then fold in the rest.

6. Spoon into a soufflé dish and bake for 45 minutes, or until the soufflé is well risen, firm to the touch in the center, and browning at the side. Serve at once.

Baked Zucchini Molds

—◆—

Serve these delicately flavored vegetable molds with a light tomato sauce.

1 onion, finely chopped
1 garlic clove, crushed
2 tablespoons olive oil
1 lb zucchini, diced
1 oz bread, without the crusts

1/3 cup milk
1 tablespoon chopped fresh basil
1 teaspoon chopped fresh mint
salt and freshly ground black pepper
2 eggs, beaten

1. Preheat the oven to 350°F.

2. In a pan, fry the onion and garlic in the oil until transparent. Add the zucchini and continue frying over low heat for about 15 minutes, stirring occasionally.

3. Mix together the bread, milk, basil, mint, salt, and pepper in a bowl. Let stand.

4. When the zucchini is cooked, mash the bread and milk with a fork. Stir in the eggs and then the zucchini mixture.

5. Spoon into individual ramekins or a large mold and place in a baking tin filled with hot water. Bake for 50-60 minutes, or until set through the center.

Stuffed Grape Leaves

—◆—

This stuffing can also be used to stuff the leaves of bok choy or large spinach leaves. For either of these alternatives, cook in more tomato juice and less oil.

SERVES 6

1/2 small onion, very finely sliced
4 tablespoons olive oil, divided
1/2 cup long-grain rice
1 cup water or vegetable stock
  (see page x)
1 tablespoon chopped raisins
2 tablespoons pine nuts

3 tablespoons chopped fresh parsley
1 teaspoon chopped fresh mint
juice of 1 lemon
salt and freshly ground black pepper
24 grape leaves
1 tablespoon tomato juice

1. In a large saucepan, fry the onion in 1 tablespoon of the oil until soft. Add the rice and stir well. Add the water or stock, raisins, nuts, parsley, and mint. Bring to a boil, stir once, and cover with a lid. Simmer for 12 minutes. Add the lemon juice and season with salt and pepper. Set aside.

2. Meanwhile, blanch the grape leaves by plunging them into boiling water for 3 minutes, then refreshing them in cold water. Drain the leaves and cut off the stalks.

3. Place a small spoonful of the rice mixture on each leaf and roll up, tucking the ends in like a parcel.

4. Stack in a small pan. Add the remaining oil, tomato juice, and sufficient water to cover. Weight a small saucer on top of the stuffed leaves so they don't float. Cover and simmer for 45 minutes. Let cool without removing the lid. When serving, discard the liquid.

Stuffed Chinese Leaves

—◆—

This recipe was inspired by a Polish recipe for stuffed cabbage, and the ingredients go well with the stronger flavor of the leaves of bok choy.

SERVES 4-6

1 head of bok choy leaves
1/4 cup long-grain rice
3 tomatoes, peeled (see page xi)
  and chopped
1/4 cup chopped mixed nuts
  (almonds, hazelnuts, walnuts)

1 onion, finely chopped
3 tablespoons chopped fresh parsley
salt and freshly ground black pepper
2 cups vegetable stock
  (see page x)
juice of 1 lemon

1. Remove 12 of the large outer bok choy leaves and blanch by plunging them into boiling water for 1 minute, then refreshing them in cold water. Drain.

2. Mix the rice, tomatoes, nuts, onions, and parsley in a bowl and season with salt and pepper. Place 1 tablespoon of the filling on each leaf and roll up neatly, being careful not to tear it.

3. Shred the remaining bok choy leaves and place them on the bottom of a wide saucepan. Carefully arrange the stuffed leaves on top.

4. Pour the stock and lemon juice over the top of the stuffed leaves. Bring to a boil, cover, and simmer for 30 minutes.

Mexican Tostadas

— ◆ —

If you like your tomato sauce as hot as the Mexicans do, add more chile.

Sauce
1 tablespoon olive or other
  vegetable oil
1 large onion, sliced
1 green pepper, seeded and chopped
1/2 red pepper, seeded and chopped
1/2-1 green chile, seeded and
  finely chopped
1 tablespoon tomato purée
1/4 teaspoon ground cumin
pinch of sugar

Filling
2 tablespoons olive or other
  vegetable oil, divided
1 small onion, thinly sliced
1 15 1/2-oz can of red kidney beans,
  drained
salt and freshly ground black pepper

12 corn tortillas
1/2 cup grated cheddar cheese
6 lettuce leaves, shredded

1. Preheat the oven to 350°F.

2. To make the sauce, heat 1 tablespoon of the oil in a pan and fry the onion, peppers, and chile for 3-4 minutes. Add the remaining sauce ingredients. Bring the mixture to a boil and simmer, covered, for 45 minutes. Take off the lid and boil to reduce any excess liquid. The sauce should be quite thick.

3. To make the filling, heat the oil in a frying pan and fry the onion until well browned. Add the drained beans and season with salt and pepper. Mash with a potato masher and cook for 2-3 minutes on one side until browned. Turn over and brown the other side. Keep warm.

4. Heat the tortillas in the oven covered with foil. Place one on each of 4 individual plates and smother with the fried beans. Add another tostada and cover with the sauce. Top with the remaining tostadas and sprinkle with cheese and lettuce. Serve at once.

Vegetable Moussaka

—◆—

SERVES 4-6

4 tablespoons vegetable oil, divided
2 large onions, sliced
4 large tomatoes, peeled (see page xi)
  and chopped
1 tablespoon tomato purée
1/4 teaspoon dried thyme
1/2 teaspoon ground coriander
salt and freshly ground black pepper

1/2 cup vegetable stock (see page x)
  or water
2 eggplants, sliced
salt
1 1/2 lbs potatoes, peeled and sliced
4 tablespoons butter
1/4 cup flour
1 1/2 cups milk or soy milk
2 eggs, beaten

1. Preheat the oven to 400°F and grease a large soufflé or casserole dish.

2. Heat 2 tablespoons of the oil in a saucepan and fry the onions until lightly browned. Add the tomatoes, tomato purée, thyme, and coriander, and season with salt and pepper. Stir, and add the stock or water. Bring to a boil, reduce the heat, and simmer for 15-20 minutes.

3. Meanwhile, place the eggplant in a shallow dish and sprinkle each slice with salt. Let stand for 15 minutes.

4. Parboil the sliced potatoes in a little salted water for about 8 minutes, being careful not to let them get too soft. Drain well.

5. Wash the eggplant and squeeze dry. Fry in the remaining oil until lightly browned on each side.

6. To assemble the moussaka, layer the potatoes, eggplant, and tomato mixture in the soufflé or casserole dish.

7. Heat the butter in a saucepan and stir in the flour. Add the milk and bring to a boil, stirring constantly. Cook for 3 minutes. Remove from the heat and beat in the eggs. Season to taste.

8. Pour this sauce over the top of the moussaka, and bake in the center of the oven for about 50-60 minutes, or until the top is set and light brown in color. Serve at once.

Carrot Coulibiac

—◆—

This vegetarian version of a Russian specialty can be made with parsnips or rutabaga in place of the carrots. It will taste good but not look as colorful. If you use tofu in place of cheese, you may need to add a little stock to moisten the mixture.

1 lb carrots, grated
1 large onion, thinly sliced
2 tablespoons butter
1 tablespoon vegetable oil
1/2 lb low-fat soft cheese or tofu
salt and freshly ground black pepper

1/3 cup long-grain rice
1/3 cup water
1/4 cup frozen peas
1 lb frozen pastry, thawed
1 1/2 lbs fresh spinach or 1/2-lb
  package of leaf spinach, thawed
grated nutmeg

1. Preheat the oven to 400°F.

2. In a saucepan, fry the carrots and onion in the butter and oil for 6-8 minutes, or until soft. Do not allow the mixture to brown. Stir in the cheese or tofu and season with salt and pepper.

3. Place the rice in a pan with the water and peas and bring to a boil. Reduce the heat, cover, and simmer for 15 minutes, or until the rice is tender and all the liquid has been absorbed. Remove from the heat and season to taste.

4. Steam the fresh spinach and drain it, or drain the frozen spinach.

5. Roll out the pastry to form a rectangle about 12 x 10 inches. Pile half the rice mixture down the center. Carefully arrange half the spinach leaves over the top. Sprinkle with nutmeg, spoon on the carrot mixture, then cover with the remaining spinach leaves and a little more nutmeg. Top with the rest of the rice mixture. Fold the pastry over the top and seal the ends with water.

6. Place the sealed side down on a greased baking tin and cook for 30-35 minutes, or until golden. Cut into slices and serve.

Tofu and Vegetable Satay

The contrasting colors of the white tofu, green fennel, green pepper, and black prunes make an attractive display. Serve on a bed of plain rice with the sauce on the side.

1/2 lb tofu, cut into 8 chunks
4 tablespoons vegetable oil
1 tablespoon grated fresh ginger
4 scallions, chopped
1 garlic clove, chopped

Satay sauce
1/4 cup coconut cream
1 tablespoon soy sauce

1 tablespoon lemon juice
3 tablespoons peanut butter
water

2 green peppers, seeded and
* quartered*
2 heads of fennel, quartered
8 prunes, pitted

1. Place the tofu in a shallow dish. Mix the oil, ginger, scallions, and garlic in a bowl and pour over the top of the tofu. Let stand until required.

2. Meanwhile, make the sauce by simmering the coconut cream in a pan with the soy sauce and lemon juice. Beat in the peanut butter and sufficient water to produce a thin cream. Heat until the sauce is thickened, adding more water if necessary.

3. Blanch the peppers and fennel by plunging them into boiling water for 4-5 minutes. Drain. Thread onto 4 skewers with the tofu and prunes. Place under a medium broiler and cook for 6-8 minutes, turning occasionally.

Vegetarian *Thali*

—◆—

In India a selection of curried vegetable dishes is often served as a vegetarian *thali* or platter. The dishes are served in small stainless steel bowls on a stainless steel tray. Choose from Okra Tamatar (see below), Tarka Dhal (see page 97), Spiced Potatoes (see page 85), Aloo Gobi (see page 101), Vegetable Curry (see page 141), and Aloo Kofta (see below), together with rice and pickles.

Okra Tamatar

4 tablespoons vegetable oil
1/2 lb okra, cut into 1-inch pieces
2 green chiles, seeded and finely
 sliced

1 jar curry sauce
pinch of salt
2 tomatoes

1. Heat the oil in a frying pan and fry the okra and chiles for 5 minutes, turning occasionally. Add the curry sauce and salt. Simmer for 3 minutes.

2. Chop the tomatoes and add them to the sauce. Mix well and serve.

Aloo Kofta

1 lb potatoes, peeled, boiled,
 and mashed
1 tablespoon mild curry paste
pinch of salt
1/8 cup chopped toasted almonds
 (see page xi)
1 teaspoon crushed fennel seeds
2 teaspoons chopped fresh cilantro
flour
vegetable oil for deep-frying

Sauce
4 tablespoons vegetable oil
1 medium onion, finely chopped
2 tomatoes, finely chopped
1/2 teaspoon grated fresh ginger
1/2 teaspoon crushed garlic
1 packet mild curry sauce mix
1/2 cup water

1. Mix together the mashed potatoes, curry paste, salt, almonds, fennel seeds, and cilantro.

2. Divide the mixture into 8 parts. Flour your hands and work each piece into an oval tube shape.

3. Deep-fry the kofta balls in fairly hot oil for approximately 5 minutes, or until brown.

4. To make the sauce, heat the oil in a saucepan and fry the onion, tomatoes, ginger, garlic, and curry sauce mix for 5 minutes. Add the water and stir until the mixture thickens. Pour over the kofta balls and serve.

Vegetable Curry

—◆—

Serve this easy-to-make but tasty curry with rice, Raita (see page 169), and Tarka Dhal (see page 97), or as part of a Vegetarian Thali (see opposite).

3 tablespoons vegetable oil
1 large onion, finely chopped
3 garlic cloves, chopped
1 1/2 lbs mixed vegetables
(carrots, cauliflower, zucchini,
eggplant, potatoes)
2 tablespoons grated fresh ginger
1 tablespoon ground cumin

1 tablespoon ground coriander
salt and freshly ground black pepper
1/2 cup water
1 cup peas
3-4 tablespoons chopped fresh cilantro
1 teaspoon garam masala or curry
powder
juice of 1/2 lemon
3 tomatoes, quartered

1. Heat the oil in a pan and fry the onion and garlic until lightly browned. Add the vegetables and stir well. Add the ginger, cumin, and coriander, and season with salt and pepper. Cook until the vegetables are lightly browned all over.

2. Pour in the water and bring to a boil. Simmer for 30 minutes.

3. Add the remaining ingredients except the tomatoes. Stir, and bring to a boil.

4. Place the tomatoes on the top. Cover and simmer for another 10 minutes.

Red Pepper Gougère

—◆—

The choux pastry for the gougère is much easier to make than you might think. The secret lies in beating in the eggs as quickly as possible. Don't worry if the mixture is a little loose.

SERVES 4-6

Filling
1 large onion, sliced
1 tablespoon vegetable oil
pat of butter
2 large red peppers, seeded and cut into strips
1 tablespoon tomato purée
1 large tomato, peeled (see page xi) and chopped
1 tablespoon chopped fresh parsley
chopped fresh rosemary or basil
salt and freshly ground black pepper

Gougère
1/2 cup water
1/4 lb butter
1/2 cup flour
pinch of salt
4 eggs
3 oz Gruyère cheese, grated
1 tablespoon grated Parmesan cheese

1. To make the filling, in a saucepan fry the onion in oil and butter until transparent. Add the pepper strips and continue frying 3-4 more minutes. Add the remaining filling ingredients and simmer for 20-30 minutes, or until thick and tender. Remove the lid and boil to reduce any excess liquid. Let cool.

2. Preheat the oven to 425°F.

3. To make the gougère, heat the water and butter in a saucepan. When the butter melts, bring the mixture to a boil and beat in the flour and salt. Remove from the heat when the mixture starts to come away from the sides of the pan. Beat in the eggs, one at a time, and continue beating until the mixture is satin-smooth. Beat in the Gruyère cheese.

4. Use the gougère mixture to line the sides of an oval baking dish, leaving the center base clear. Fill this hollow with the pepper mixture, sprinkle with Parmesan, and bake for 1 hour and 10 minutes. Check after 50 minutes, and cover with foil for the last 15 minutes if it's browning too quickly.

Avocado Risotto with Mexican Sauce

—◆—

The contrasting colors and flavors of this dish make an unusual main course for a dinner party. Serve a tossed green salad with olive oil and lemon juice on the side.

Mexican sauce
1 red pepper, seeded and
  finely chopped
1 green pepper, seeded and
  finely chopped
1 garlic clove, crushed
1 tablespoon vegetable oil
8 tomatoes, chopped
1 teaspoon ground coriander
2 cloves
1/2 teaspoon chili powder
1 cup vegetable stock (see page x)
  or water
salt and freshly ground black pepper

Risotto
1 large onion, finely chopped
1 tablespoon olive oil
1 1/2 cups Italian arborio rice
1 cup white wine
2 avocados, chopped
4 tablespoons raisins
1/2 teaspoon dried mixed herbs
salt and freshly ground black pepper
2 cups vegetable stock (see page x)

1. To make the sauce, in a saucepan fry the peppers and garlic in the oil for 5 minutes. Add the remaining sauce ingredients, season with salt and pepper, and bring to a boil. Simmer for 20 minutes. Put the sauce in a blender to make it smooth, and correct the seasoning, if necessary.

2. To make the risotto, in a saucepan fry the onion in the oil until transparent. Add the rice and continue frying for 3-4 minutes. Add the wine and bring to a boil. Continue cooking until the wine is absorbed, stirring occasionally.

3. Add the avocados, raisins, herbs, salt, pepper, and stock. Continue cooking about 20-30 minutes, or until the rice has absorbed all the stock, stirring occasionally. Add more stock if the rice is too dry.

4. Reheat the sauce and serve with the risotto.

Ratatouille Roulade

— ♦ —

The soufflé-like mixture bakes to a firm rectangle which is not difficult to roll once the ratatouille filling is in place. It looks wonderful, and it's a really impressive dish to serve at a dinner party.

Ratatouille filling
1/2 lb onions, chopped
1/2 lb zucchini, sliced
1/2 lb tomatoes, chopped
1 eggplant, diced
1 green pepper, seeded and diced
1 tablespoon vegetable oil
2 tablespoons tomato purée
1/2 cup dry white wine
1/2 teaspoon dried oregano

salt and freshly ground black pepper
1/2 tablespoon flour

Roulade
1 tablespoon butter
1 tablespoon flour
1/2 cup milk
5 eggs, separated
salt and freshly ground black pepper

1. To make the filling, in a saucepan fry all the vegetables in the oil. After 3-4 minutes add the tomato purée, wine, and oregano. Season with salt and pepper and bring to a boil. Sprinkle on the flour and stir. Cook for about 30 minutes, or until all the vegetables are soft and most of the liquid has evaporated.

2. Preheat the oven to 400°F. Line a 10- x 14-inch Swiss roll tin with parchment paper. Oil the paper well.

3. To make the roulade, place the butter, flour, and milk in a saucepan and whisk over low heat until the mixture thickens. Beat well, add the egg yolks, and season with salt and pepper.

4. In a bowl, whisk the egg whites until really stiff. Carefully fold them into the roulade base and pour into the lined tin. Bake for 15 minutes.

5. Remove from the oven and pour two-thirds of the ratatouille mixture over the roulade. Roll up, removing the wax paper as you go. Serve with the remaining ratatouille on either side.

Asparagus Pancake Stack

— ◆ —

I find that this is a good dinner party dish because I can make both the pancakes and filling well in advance. You can use fresh or frozen asparagus. Just cook the asparagus first and chop it.

Pancakes
1/2 cup flour
pinch of salt
2 eggs, separated
1 cup milk
vegetable oil

Filling
3 tablespoons flour
3 tablespoons butter

1 12-oz can of asparagus, drained
and chopped, retaining the liquid
milk
1/2 cup dry white wine
salt and freshly ground black pepper
1/2 lb mushrooms, finely chopped
2 tablespoons vegetable oil

chopped fresh parsley

1. To make the pancakes, mix the flour, salt, egg yolks, and milk in a bowl. In another bowl, whisk the egg whites until really stiff and fold into the flour mixture. Grease an 8-inch frying pan with oil and heat. Spoon one-fourth of the batter into the hot pan to make a thick pancake. Cook until golden, then turn over and cook the other side. Repeat to make 3 more pancakes. Keep warm while you make the filling.

2. To make the filling, place the flour and butter in a pan. Measure the liquid from the can of asparagus and add enough milk to make 2 cups of fluid. Add to the flour and butter and whisk over medium heat until thickened. Add the wine, and season with salt and pepper. The sauce should be fairly thick.

3. To half of the sauce, add the chopped asparagus. In a saucepan, fry the mushrooms in the oil and add them to the other half of the sauce.

4. To make the stack, lay one pancake on a serving dish and cover with half the mushroom sauce. Add another pancake and cover with half the asparagus sauce. Continue alternating layers, ending with asparagus. Decorate with parsley and serve at once. Cut like a cake.

BUFFET FOOD

Choose two or three of the pastry-based dishes in this section, and team them up with a selection of salads for a really impressive buffet. Ideas include Watercress Flan, Savory Pumpkin Plait, and Rice Cake with Carrot and Fennel Coleslaw and Sala Beet Salad; Pâtés de Béziers and Onion and Black Olive Tart with Cauliflower and Grilled Red Pepper Salad and Mixed Leaf and Pistachio Nut Salad; or St. Christopher Savory Roll, Celery Root and Carrot Flan, and Rainbow Pasta Salad with Cauliflower Salad and Whole-Wheat Rolls.

A good winter buffet includes Hot Cauliflower Terrine, Smoked Tofu Kedgeree, and Mexican Baked Spinach; or Indian Chickpeas, Singapore Rice, and Roman-Style Spinach.

All the pasta and stir-fry dishes in earlier chapters can be increased in volume and served as buffet food. Finish off with a large bowl of fruit.

Cheese Log

Use any well-flavored, firm, mature cheese for this dish.

SERVES 16

1 1/2 lbs cheese, grated
3/4 lb carrots or celery root, grated
6 tablespoons chopped scallion
4 tablespoons chopped fresh parsley

6 tablespoons mayonnaise
salt and freshly ground black pepper
fresh herb sprigs
cherry tomatoes

1. Mix the cheese with the carrots or celery root, scallion, parsley, and mayonnaise in a bowl. Season with salt and pepper.

2. Spoon the mixture down the center of a large rectangle of wax paper and roll up into a log shape. Place in the refrigerator to cool for 1 hour.

3. Carefully remove the paper and serve garnished with sprigs of fresh herbs and cherry tomatoes. Cut into slices to serve.

Watercress Flan

—◆—

Cook the flan base in advance, and fill just before serving. Cottage cheese or grated cheddar can also be used in place of tofu.

SERVES 12

3/4 lb pastry (enough for 2 crusts)
2 bunches watercress, divided
8 celery stalks, chopped
1 bunch scallions, finely chopped

1 lb tofu, mashed
3-4 tablespoons mayonnaise
salt and freshly ground black pepper
1/2 cup walnuts, chopped

1. Preheat the oven to 400°F.

2. Roll out the pastry and use it to line two 8-inch flan tins. Prick the bases all over with a fork and line with foil and dried beans. Bake for about 15 minutes, then remove the foil and beans. Cook 15 more minutes, or until done. Remove from the oven and let cool.

3. Retain 12 sprigs of watercress from the bunches and reserve for garnish. Coarsely chop the rest and use to line the cooled pastry-lined flan tins.

4. Mix the celery, scallions, tofu, and mayonnaise in a bowl. Season with salt and pepper. Spoon into the center of the flan tins, leaving a little of the watercress showing around the edges.

5. Place the walnuts around the edges on top of the watercress, and decorate the center with the reserved sprigs of watercress. Serve at once.

Pâtés de Béziers

—◆—

These attractive little tartlets from the Languedoc can be made with almost any kind of dough. In France they are usually covered with pastry lids, but these open versions look more attractive.

SERVES 16

Pastry
3/4 cup butter or firm margarine
1 1/4 cups white flour
1/2 teaspoon salt
1 egg, beaten
2 tablespoons water

Chèvre tomato filling
1/2 lb chèvre
4 tablespoons goat milk yogurt
  or cow's milk yogurt
1 egg

leaves from 2-3 fresh thyme sprigs
salt and freshly ground black pepper
3 tomatoes, sliced

Onion filling
1 lb onions, sliced
2 tablespoons olive oil
1 egg, beaten
1/3 lb low-fat semi-soft cheese
  or cottage cheese
1/2 teaspoon dried sage
salt and freshly ground black pepper

1. To make the pastry, rub the butter or margarine into the flour and salt until the mixture resembles rough breadcrumbs. Bind with the beaten egg and water. Leave in the refrigerator for 2 hours. You can also use prepared frozen or refrigerated pastry dough.

2. Roll out the dough and use it to line sixteen 4-inch flan tins.

3. Preheat the oven to 375°F.

4. To make the chèvre filling, cut the rind off the cheese and beat with the yogurt to make a smooth cream. Then beat in the egg, thyme, salt, and pepper.

5. Place the tomato slices in the base of the 8 prepared flan tins, and spoon the cheese mixture over the top. Bake for 35 minutes.

6. To make the onion filling, in a small pan fry the onions in the oil until softened. Beat the egg and cheese together and stir in the onion and sage. Season with salt and pepper. Spoon into the remaining 8 pastry-lined flan tins and bake for 35 minutes.

Celery Root and Carrot Flan

—◆—

This potato pastry can be used for any kind of quiche or savory tart. For the best results, chill the pastry for half an hour before cooking.

SERVES 6-8

Potato pastry
4 tablespoons firm margarine
1/3 cup cold mashed potato
1/2 cup whole-wheat flour
1 teaspoon baking powder
pinch of salt

Filling
1/2 lb celery root, sliced
1 large carrot, grated
3 eggs
1/2 cup yogurt
1/4 cup skim milk
2 oz cheddar cheese, grated
salt and freshly ground black pepper

1. Preheat the oven to 375°F.

2. To make the pastry, cream the margarine with the back of a spoon. Use a fork to work in the potato, flour, baking powder, and salt. Blend well together and turn onto a floured board. Knead slightly, and roll out to fill the base of an 8-inch flan tin. Work the pastry up the sides of the pan with your fingers and place in the refrigerator for half an hour.

3. To make the filling, cook the celery root in boiling water for 10 minutes. Drain and grate. Mix with the grated carrot. Beat the eggs, yogurt, and milk together in a bowl and stir in the cheese and vegetables. Season with salt and pepper.

4. Spoon into the flan base, spread evenly, and bake for about 45 minutes, or until set in the center and golden brown.

Onion and Black Olive Tart

—◆—

This well-flavored tart from Provence makes a good buffet dish. It is traditionally made with a yeast dough. However, if you are in a hurry, the pastry is quicker to make.

SERVES 6-8

Yeast dough
1 1/4 cups flour
1/2 teaspoon salt
1 1/2 teaspoons activated dried yeast
2 1/2 tablespoons olive oil
3/4 cup lukewarm water

Topping
3 tablespoons olive oil
3 lbs onions, sliced
salt and freshly ground black pepper
24 black olives, pitted

Alternative pastry dough
6 tablespoons butter
1 cup flour
1/4 teaspoon salt
1/4 cup water

1. If you are making the yeast dough, in a bowl mix the flour with the salt and yeast. Add the oil and sufficient water to make a fairly stiff dough. Knead on a floured surface for 10 minutes then let rise in a warm place in a greased mixing bowl covered with plastic wrap.

2. If you are making the pastry dough base, rub the butter into the flour and salt until the mixture resembles breadcrumbs. Bind with water and knead lightly to form a dough.

3. To make the topping, heat the oil in a pan and add the onions. Stir until the onions soften, then let it simmer. The onions should not brown, but in about 40 minutes will slowly melt to a golden purée. Season with salt and pepper.

4. Preheat the oven to 425°F.

5. Roll out your chosen dough and use it to line a 10-inch flan tin. Spoon the onion mixture into the tin, dot with olives, and bake in the oven for 30-35 minutes, or until the base is cooked through.

Savory Pumpkin Plait

—◆—

The smoked tofu gives a distinctive flavor to this attractive puff pastry buffet dish.

SERVES 8-10

1/3 lb smoked tofu, diced
1 cup pumpkin, diced
1 small onion, chopped
2 lbs potatoes, peeled and diced
1 small carrot, diced
3 tablespoons frozen peas
1 teaspoon dried mixed herbs

1 tablespoon chopped fresh parsley
salt and freshly ground black pepper
2 tablespoons vegetable oil
1 13-oz packet of frozen puff pastry,
  thawed
1 egg, beaten

1. Preheat the oven to 425°F.

2. Mix the tofu with the vegetables, herbs, and parsley in a bowl. Season with salt and pepper. Heat the oil in a pan and fry the vegetable mixture for 8 minutes.

3. Roll out the pastry to approximately 3 x 11 inches and trim to a neat oblong. Arrange the cooked vegetables down the center, leaving 4 inches of pastry clear at each side. Make slanting cuts into the base pastry on each side, about 1 inch apart. Criss-cross these pieces alternately to enclose the filling. Neaten the ends and place on a baking sheet.

4. Brush with the egg and bake for 20 minutes. Reduce the heat to 350°F and bake 15 more minutes.

St. Christopher Savory Roll

—◆—

This was one of the first dishes I ever learned to cook at school, and I am still using it as a centerpiece for a hot buffet.

SERVES 5-6

Filling
1 cup grated cheddar cheese
2 onions, finely chopped
2 tablespoons tomato purée
salt and freshly ground black pepper

Pastry
6 tablespoons butter
1 cup flour
pinch of salt
water

1. Preheat the oven to 400°F.

2. Mix all the filling ingredients together in a bowl and set aside.

3. To make the pastry, rub the butter into the flour and salt to make a breadcrumb mixture. Bind with a little water. Roll out to a 10- x 12-inch rectangle.

4. Spread the cheese mixture over the pastry, leaving a small margin clear around the edges. Roll up the pastry and filling from the long side to form a flat-shaped Swiss roll. Place on an oiled baking tray in a crescent shape.

5. Cut across the roll, leaving the pastry uncut at one side, to make about 12 sections. Starting from one end, partially twist each of the sections to expose the filling. Bake for about 25-30 minutes. Serve hot or cold.

Cardamom Cheese Pie

—◆—

The filling for this dish was inspired by very typical Chilean ingredients—raisins, sugar, and eggs—and they work very well in this party pie.

SERVES 8-10

Pastry
1/2 lb butter
1 cup flour
pinch of salt
water

Filling
8 hard-boiled eggs
1/2 cup grated cheddar cheese
1 cup raisins
2 tablespoons sugar
crushed seeds from 2 cardamom pods

1. Preheat the oven to 400°F.

2. To make the pastry, rub the butter into the flour and salt, and bind with a little water. Roll out the dough and use three-fourths of it to line two 8-inch flan tins.

3. To make the filling, chop the hard-boiled eggs and mix with the remaining ingredients. Spoon into the pastry-lined flan tins.

4. Roll out the remaining pastry to make lids. Apply the lids, fork the edges, and prick the center. Bake for 45 minutes, or until the pastry is cooked.

Rice Cake

This colorful rice salad looks great on a serving dish surrounded by watercress.

SERVES 12

1 lb long-grain rice
1 cup sour cream
1 cup grated cooked beets
4 hard-boiled eggs, chopped

1/3 cup chopped peanuts
salt and freshly ground black pepper
1/2 bunch watercress

1. Cook the rice in double its volume of boiling salted water. Drain well and fluff up with a fork. Stir in the sour cream and let cool.

2. Mix the beets, eggs, and peanuts in a bowl. Add the cooled rice and season with salt and pepper.

3. Pack into a loaf pan and weight the top. Chill well, unmold, and serve garnished with watercress.

Vegetable Terrine

—◆—

This terrine is as colorful as it is delicious. It looks great on a buffet, or it can be served as the first course at a special dinner.

SERVES 8

1 lb carrots, chopped
1 lb parsnips, chopped
2 tablespoons butter
1 medium onion, chopped
6 eggs, divided
4 tablespoons strained yogurt, divided

salt and freshly ground black pepper
2 lbs fresh spinach, tough stalks removed, or 1 lb frozen chopped spinach
1/2 teaspoon grated nutmeg
2 tablespoons chopped chives

1. Put the carrots and parsnips into separate saucepans with enough boiling water to half-cover the vegetables. Cook until *al dente*. Drain both well.

2. In a small pan, melt the butter, add the onion, and cook until softened.

3. In a bowl, beat 2 eggs with 2 tablespoons of yogurt, season with salt and pepper, and whisk together until smooth.

4. Put the carrots into a food processor with half the cooked onions, and purée to the stage where the mixture is still fairly coarse. Turn into a bowl and stir in the eggs and yogurt mixture. Spoon this carrot mixture into the base of a well-greased loaf pan.

5. Repeat the same procedure with the parsnips, using the rest of the onion, 2 eggs, and the remaining yogurt, then carefully spoon over the carrot layer.

6. Preheat the oven to 350°F.

7. Put the fresh spinach into a large saucepan of water, place over medium-high heat, and cook for a few minutes until wilted. Turn into a colander and squeeze out as much water as possible. Finely chop on a board or in a food processor.

8. Add the remaining beaten eggs, the nutmeg, and chives to the chopped spinach and season with salt and pepper. Spoon this mixture over the parsnip layer, then cover with a piece of well-buttered wax paper.

9. Place the loaf pan in a baking dish and pour in enough water to fill the dish about to the top. Cook in the oven for 1 1/4 hours. Allow to cool for 10 minutes before serving. Slice carefully.

Hot Cauliflower Terrine

This was one of the first vegetarian dishes I ever tried out on my meat-eating friends, and they could not believe that vegetarian food could be so good!

SERVES 8-10

2 cauliflower heads
2 onions, chopped
2 tablespoons butter or
  firm margarine
3/4 cup fresh breadcrumbs

1 cup sour cream
4 eggs, beaten
pinch of grated nutmeg
salt and freshly ground black pepper
chopped fresh parsley

1. Preheat the oven to 375°F. Grease a large casserole or soufflé dish.

2. Remove the outer leaves and excess stalks from the cauliflower and steam until tender. Drain well and mash to a purée.

3. In a saucepan, fry the onions in butter until softened. Mix in the mashed cauliflower, breadcrumbs, sour cream, eggs, and nutmeg. Season with salt and pepper.

4. Spoon the mixture into the prepared casserole or soufflé dish and bake for 1 hour. Sprinkle the top with parsley and serve at once.

Smoked Tofu Kedgeree

—◆—

If you do not want to include eggs, substitute 1 pound of cooked vegetables such as cubed celery root or chopped artichoke hearts with some diced carrots or sweet corn for color.

SERVES 8

1/2 cup butter or firm margarine
1 1/2 lbs cooked long-grain
  brown rice
1 1/2 lbs smoked tofu, cubed
6 hard-boiled eggs, chopped

pinch of curry powder
salt and freshly ground black pepper
1 cup sour cream or puréed silken
  tofu
8 tablespoons chopped fresh parsley

1. Heat the butter or margarine in a deep saucepan and toss in the rice, stirring until the rice is thoroughly coated. Add the tofu and eggs, and fold carefully into the rice.

2. Mix the remaining ingredients in a cup and pour over the kedgeree. Warm through, stirring, and serve at once.

Mexican Baked Spinach

—◆—

This is a favorite of mine for buffet parties. Serve with Texan Rice (see page 63), Stewed Beets with Onions (see page 90), and another vegetable dish of your choice.

SERVES 12

2 3/4 lbs spinach, tough stalks
  removed
4 green peppers, seeded and sliced
2 large onions, finely chopped
1/2 head celery, finely chopped
2 tablespoons vegetable oil
1/2 cup raisins

1 teaspoon ground cinnamon
1/2 teaspoon cayenne
1/2 teaspoon dill seeds
salt and freshly ground black pepper
1/2 cup tomato juice
1 cup grated cheese

1. Preheat the oven to 375°F.

2. Steam the spinach in a large pan with no added water for 5 minutes, or until soft. Blanch the green peppers for 5 minutes in boiling water.

3. In a saucepan, fry the onions and celery in the oil with the raisins, cinnamon, cayenne, and dill seed for 5 minutes.

4. Place half the spinach in the base of a large oval earthenware dish. Season with salt and pepper and sprinkle with a little tomato juice. Add a layer of peppers and then all the onion-celery mixture. Season and sprinkle with more tomato juice and half the cheese. Cover with the remaining peppers. Add the remaining spinach, season, and sprinkle with the remaining tomato juice. Top with the remaining cheese. Bake for 45 minutes.

Indian Chickpeas

——◆——

This dish is based on an old recipe from Delhi. It can be made hotter by adding fresh green chiles.

SERVES 8-10

3 tablespoons vegetable oil
2 teaspoons whole coriander seeds
1 teaspoon whole cumin seeds
1 onion, sliced
2 garlic cloves, chopped
2 teaspoons ground coriander

1 teaspoon each of ground cumin and turmeric
1 14-oz can of tomatoes
2 teaspoons paprika
1 teaspoon salt
2 14-oz cans of chickpeas, drained
1 teaspoon grated ginger

1. Heat the oil in a heavy-bottomed saucepan and fry the whole spices for 1 minute. Add the onion and garlic and continue frying for 2-3 minutes.

2. Add the ground spices. Stir, and add the remaining ingredients except the ginger. Bring the mixture to a boil, cover, and simmer for 20 minutes.

3. Add the ginger and cook for 5 more minutes, or until fairly thick.

Rainbow Pasta Salad

—◆—

Use a packet of three-colored pasta spirals for the best effect.

SERVES 10

*1/2 lb mixed plain, tomato, and
  spinach pasta spirals*
salt
4 1/2 tablespoons olive oil, divided
*1 tablespoon cider or white
  wine vinegar*
1 bunch scallions, finely chopped

1 green pepper, seeded and diced
1 red pepper, seeded and diced
3 tablespoons cooked corn
pinch of mixed dried herbs
freshly ground black pepper
8 black olives, pitted and halved

1. Cook the pasta as directed on the package in boiling salted water with 1 teaspoon of the oil. When the pasta is just tender, drain well.

2. Toss in the rest of the oil and vinegar and let cool.

3. Add the remaining ingredients. Toss well and serve.

FINGER FOOD

—◆—

This section includes recipes for some of my favorite finger food. I like some of the recipes so much that I make them for everything—from dinner party appetizers to everyday snacks. The pâtés and spreads also make good sandwich fillings or toppings for toasted bread.

A good selection of canapés for a two-hour cocktail party includes Green Goddess Dip with Celery, Peanut and Garlic Pâté Canapés, Chopped Egg and Onion on Rye, Cheese Dreams, Aioli in Mushroom Caps, and Sesame Balls. A more substantial finger-food menu for an evening party includes Guacamole with Potato Skins, Mali Canapés, Stuffed Eggs, Chinese Money Bags, Tofu Cakes with Sweet-Sour Sauce, and Spiced Lentil Tartlets.

Peanut and Garlic Pâté

—◆—

This makes a good spread for fried bread canapés. Top some with capers and others with diced tomato or sliced stuffed olives.

MAKES 24-30

3 tablespoons peanut butter
1/4 lb soft cheese
2-3 garlic cloves, finely chopped

2 tablespoons yogurt
dash of tabasco
salt and freshly ground black pepper

1. Place all the ingredients in a bowl and mix together with a fork until well blended.

2. Store in the refrigerator until required.

Green Goddess Dip with Celery

—◆—

This recipe came from a friend in Washington state. If you use a little less mayonnaise you can spread the mixture directly onto the sticks of celery instead of serving as a dip.

SERVES 20

6-8 young spinach leaves,
very finely shredded
1/2 lb low-fat soft cheese
2 1/2 tablespoons mayonnaise
1 garlic clove, crushed

chopped green tips from a bunch of
scallions
chopped fresh parsley
salt and freshly ground black pepper
2 heads of celery

1. Chop the spinach and mix it with the cheese and mayonnaise in a bowl. Stir in the garlic, scallions, and parsley, and season with salt and pepper.

2. Serve with trimmed lengths of celery.

Mali Canapés

—◆—

Plain or smoked tofu can be used very successfully in place of cheese in this African-inspired recipe.

MAKES 40

1/2 cup grated cheddar cheese
4 tablespoons chopped peanuts
2 tablespoons chopped raisins
2 tablespoons mayonnaise

salt and freshly ground black pepper
8 pieces of toast
chopped parsley

1. Mix all the ingredients in a bowl except the toast and parsley. Chill for 1 hour.

2. Spread on toast. Cut each piece into 6 squares and serve sprinkled with parsley.

Guacamole with Potato Skins

—◆—

Make plenty of this, as it is extremely popular. Stop the guacamole from discoloring on top by using plenty of lemon juice and keeping it well covered with plastic wrap until the very last minute. It is the exposure to air that turns the avocado flesh black. Incidentally, the idea that leaving the avocado pit in the purée will somehow prevent the change in color is not true, so throw the pits away.

SERVES 20

8 large baked potatoes
melted butter or vegetable oil

Guacamole
juice of 2 lemons, divided
3 ripe tomatoes, finely chopped

1 small onion, finely chopped
1 small bunch of cilantro,
*   finely chopped*
salt and freshly ground black pepper
dash of tabasco
3 large ripe avocados

1. Preheat the oven to 400°F.

2. Cut each of the potatoes into 6 wedges and remove most of the flesh (reserve for use in Cheese Nut Patties, see page 106). Brush the potato skins with butter or oil and place on a baking sheet. Cook in the oven for about 10 minutes until they are crisp. Turn them regularly.

3. To make the guacamole, mix half the lemon juice in a bowl with all the ingredients except the avocados and chill until required.

4. At the last minute, peel and stone the avocados. Mash the flesh and remaining lemon juice with a fork, or purée in a blender or food processor, and stir into the tomato-onion mixture. Serve immediately with the hot potato skins.

Sesame Balls

——◆——

These highly nutritious cocktail bites have a base of feta cheese and ground seeds. They can be made in advance and stored in the refrigerator. However, it is not a good idea to leave them overnight, as they tend to dry out.

MAKES 40

1/2 cup sesame seeds
1/2 cup sunflower seeds
1/2 cup pumpkin seeds
1/4 lb feta cheese

4 teaspoons soy sauce
4 teaspoons toasted sesame oil
2 egg whites, beaten
alfalfa sprouts

1. Preheat the oven to 400°F.

2. Spread the sesame seeds on a baking tray and toast in the oven for 5-6 minutes, turning once or twice with a wooden spoon.

3. Place the sunflower and pumpkin seeds in a food processor and blend until they are smooth and almost creamy. Turn out into a bowl.

4. Add the cheese, soy sauce, and oil to the bowl and mix.

5. Shape into 40 small balls. Dip each ball in egg white and then in the sesame seeds. Serve on a bed of sprouts.

Chinese Money Bags

—◆—

Serve these crunchy wontons with their mouth-watering filling as canapés, or as part of a finger buffet. Three or four can also be served as an unusual dinner-party starter with home-made chutney. Vegans might use smoked tofu instead of blue cheese.

MAKES 24

4 sheets filo pastry
water

Filling
5 oz blue Brie, rind removed
1/4 cup chopped walnuts

6 scallions, finely chopped
grated rind of 1 orange

vegetable oil for deep-frying

1. Cut each sheet of filo pastry into twelve 4-inch squares and brush very lightly with water. Arrange in pairs so you have 24 double wrappers.

2. To make the filling, mix all the ingredients in a bowl.

3. Place 1 teaspoon of the filling on each double filo pastry square. Dampen the edges again, if necessary, and pinch together into money bag shapes.

4. Heat the oil in a deep-fryer, and check the temperature by dropping a 1-inch cube of stale bread into the oil—it should brown in 1 minute. Drop the money bags into the hot oil in batches of 5 or 6 and cook for 2-3 minutes until crisp and golden. Drain on paper towels and serve as quickly as possible.

Chopped Egg and Onion on Rye

—◆—

Use this Jewish favorite to make canapés on squares of rye bread or pumpernickel.

SERVES 24

6 hard boiled eggs, finely chopped
1 bunch scallions, finely chopped
2-3 tablespoons soft cheese
   or mayonnaise

dash of wine vinegar
salt and freshly ground black pepper
6 slices of rye or black bread

1. Mix all the ingredients except the bread in a bowl and chill until required.

2. Spread onto the pieces of bread and cut into squares.

Curried Bean and Onion Squares

—◆—

Any canned beans can be used for this spicy canapé spread, but soybeans make a particularly firm spread.

MAKES 30

4 small onions, chopped
3 tablespoons vegetable oil
1 1/2 teaspoons curry powder
2 teaspoons ground cumin
2 garlic cloves, crushed
4 tablespoons water

1 cup cooked soybeans, or drained
   canned Great Northern beans,
   puréed
7-8 large slices of buttered toast
chopped fresh parsley

1. In a saucepan, fry the onions in the oil with the curry powder, cumin, and garlic until transparent. Add the water and simmer for 5-8 minutes. Add the puréed beans and mix well. Allow to cool.

2. Spread on buttered toast. Cut into squares and serve sprinkled with parsley.

Aioli in Mushroom Caps

— ◆ —

This garlic mayonnaise can also be used to stuff cherry tomatoes or celery sticks.

MAKES 25-30

4-6 garlic cloves, crushed
1 egg yolk
2 cups olive oil
salt and freshly ground black pepper

1 tablespoon lemon juice
2 lbs button mushrooms,
  stalks removed
fresh parsley sprigs

1. To make the aioli, beat the garlic and egg yolk together and whisk in the oil very gradually to make a thick mayonnaise. Season with salt and pepper and stir in the lemon juice.

2. Fill the mushrooms with the aioli. Garnish with parsley sprigs.

Spanish Squares

— ◆ —

Because this Spanish omelette is packed with vegetables, it is a little difficult to eat with your fingers. If you are worried about your carpet, add another egg to the mixture to help bind things together.

3 potatoes, peeled
1 onion
1 tomato
1/2 green pepper, seeded

2 zucchini
2 tablespoons vegetable oil
6 eggs
salt and freshly ground black pepper

1. Dice all the vegetables very small and fry in the oil in a 9-inch frying pan for about 5 minutes.

2. Beat the eggs, season them with salt and pepper, and pour them over the vegetables. Stir well. Reduce the heat to low and allow the eggs to set for about 30 minutes.

3. Place the pan under the broiler for 10-15 minutes to brown. Let cool and cut into squares. Serve warm or cold.

Tofu Cakes with Sweet-Sour Sauce

—◆—

Cook these tasty little bites in batches and serve as soon as they are made. Larger cakes can be shallow-fried and served as part of a buffet.

MAKES 24

Sweet-sour sauce
1 1/2 cups pineapple juice
6 tablespoons cider vinegar
6 tablespoons sherry
3 tablespoons soy sauce
6 tablespoons sugar

1 lb tofu
1 bunch scallions, finely chopped

2 tablespoons grated fresh ginger
1 teaspoon grated orange rind
1/2 cup fresh breadcrumbs
2 tablespoons soy sauce
freshly ground black pepper
4 tablespoons rice flour, potato
flour, or corn flour
vegetable oil for deep-frying

1. To make the sauce, mix all the sauce ingredients together in a saucepan and boil for 6-8 minutes until it begins to thicken a little.

2. Meanwhile, mash the tofu with a fork and mix in the remaining ingredients except the flour and oil. Shape into small flat balls or cakes and dust with the flour.

3. Deep-fry in batches in hot oil for 4 minutes. Serve hot with the sweet-sour sauce.

Spiced Lentil Tartlets

—◆—

If you do not want to be bothered with making pastry cases, this spicy filling can be piled onto squares of rye bread.

MAKES 24

Filling
1 tablespoon vegetable oil
1 large onion, finely chopped
1 garlic clove, finely chopped
1 tablespoon tomato purée
1/2 teaspoon chili powder
1/4 teaspoon ground cumin
1/2 teaspoon dried thyme
1/4 teaspoon ground allspice
salt and freshly ground black pepper

1/2 cup dried split lentils
2 cups water
1 teaspoon nutritional yeast

Pastry
1/4 lb butter or firm margarine
1 cup flour
pinch of salt
water

1. To make the filling, heat the oil in a pan and fry the onion, garlic, tomato purée, chili powder, cumin, thyme, allspice, salt, and pepper for 5 minutes. Add the lentils and cover with the water and yeast extract. Simmer covered, for about 1-1 1/2 hours, or until the lentils are cooked and the mixture is fairly thick.

2. Preheat the oven to 400°F.

3. To make the pastry, rub the butter or margarine into the flour and salt until the mixture resembles fine breadcrumbs. Bind with water. Roll out three-fourths of the pastry and use to line 24 small tartlet tins. Roll out the remaining pastry to make lids.

4. Place a spoonful of the filling in each tartlet and cover with a pastry lid. Pinch closed. Bake for about 35-40 minutes, or until lightly browned. Serve hot.

Stuffed Eggs

—◆—

Stuffed eggs are always popular finger food. I like to make two or three different stuffings and mix them on a platter. Quantities I give here are for six hard-boiled eggs.

1. Watercress

1 bunch watercress, divided
1/2 cup mayonnaise

salt and freshly ground black pepper

1. Process the egg yolks until they are smooth. Finely chop the watercress, retaining a few sprigs for garnish. Add the chopped watercress to the egg yolks with the mayonnaise, season with salt and pepper, and mix well.

2. Spoon back into the egg whites and garnish with a few sprigs of watercress.

2. Curried Onion

2 tablespoons vegetable oil
1 small onion, finely chopped
1 tablespoon curry powder

2 tablespoons mango chutney,
* chopped if necessary*
mayonnaise
parsley sprigs

1. Heat the oil in a pan and fry the onion for 4-5 minutes, or until well browned. Stir in the curry powder and cook for another 2 minutes. Let cool.

2. Process the egg yolks until they are smooth. Add the chutney and a little mayonnaise.

3. Spoon back into the egg whites and garnish with a few sprigs of parsley.

3. Provençale

*1 2-oz jar of black olive paste
(or see the recipe for Tapenade
on page 170)*

*1 tablespoon chopped capers
whole capers, drained*

1. Process the egg yolks until they are smooth and mix with the olive paste and chopped capers.

2. Spoon back into the egg whites and garnish with a few whole capers.

4. Coriander and Tahini

*2 tablespoons mayonnaise
1 tablespoon tahini*

*3 tablespoons chopped fresh cilantro
salt and freshly ground black pepper*

1. Process the egg yolks until they are smooth. In a bowl, mix the mayonnaise and tahini to make a smooth soft paste. Add the egg yolks and cilantro, season with salt and pepper, and mix well.

2. Spoon back into the egg whites.

Raita

——◆——

This cooling yogurt goes well with both Indian and Middle Eastern dishes. In the Middle East garlic is added instead of cumin seeds, and the dish is served as an appetizer with hot pita bread.

*1 cup yogurt
1 small cucumber, diced or
  coarsely grated
2 tablespoons chopped fresh mint*

*1/2 teaspoon ground cumin
1/4 teaspoon cayenne
pinch of salt*

1. In a bowl, whisk the yogurt to make it really smooth and stir in all the other ingredients. Chill before serving.

Tapenade

—◆—

Though you can buy this olive paste ready-made, it is fun to make at home. Serve as a starter or snack with toasted crusty bread.

SERVES 12

1 1/2 cups black olives, pitted
2 tablespoons capers
2 garlic cloves, crushed
1 tablespoon Dijon mustard

1 tablespoon lemon juice
1 cup extra-virgin olive oil
freshly ground black pepper
toasted crusty bread

1. Put all the ingredients except the oil, pepper, and bread in a food processor or blender and roughly chop.

2. With the machine still running, gradually add the oil. Season with pepper.

3. Spoon into a serving dish and chill well for 1-2 hours. Serve with toasted bread.

Cheese Dreams

—◆—

These simple fried sandwiches are the most popular finger food I have ever served. They disappear just as fast as I can make them.

MAKES 40

soft butter
12 slices of bread
1 lb cheddar cheese, grated

4 tablespoons chutney
salt and freshly ground black pepper
butter for frying

1. Butter the bread thinly and mix the cheese and chutney together in a bowl. Season with salt and pepper.

2. Make up 6 sandwiches with the bread and the cheese mixture. Cut each sandwich into quarters and each quarter into 2 triangles.

3. Fry each triangle on both sides in hot butter and serve at once.

Orange Cheese Truffles

—◆—

This combination of dried fruit, orange juice, and soft cheese provides something for guests with a sweet tooth.

MAKES 60

1 cup dates
1 cup raisins
3/4 cup slivered almonds
1 lb cream cheese
1 teaspoon mixed ground spices
 (cinnamon, nutmeg, allspice)

rind and juice of 1 orange
3-4 tablespoons ground toasted
 sesame seeds (see page xi)
7 oranges

1. Finely chop the dates, raisins, and almonds in a processor and mix with the cream cheese. Add the spices and the finely grated rind of one orange together with enough juice from the same orange to make a stiff paste. Mix well and chill for 4-6 hours.

2. Remove from the refrigerator and shape into about 60 small balls. Roll in the sesame seeds.

3. To serve, slice remaining oranges into slim wedges and arrange on a large plate with the cheese truffles.

Garlic Sauce with Vegetables

—◆—

This rather unusual garlic sauce uses a combination of bread and ground almonds as thickening agents. Serve as a dip as part of a buffet or for a pre-dinner nibble.

SERVES 12

6 slices of day-old bread,
  crusts removed
water
4-6 garlic cloves, crushed
2 tablespoons white wine vinegar
1 cup extra-virgin olive oil

4 tablespoons ground almonds
pinch of salt
selection of lightly cooked vegetables
  (zucchini, scallions, asparagus,
  cauliflower)

1. Soak the bread in water for 5 minutes. Squeeze out all the moisture and blend with the garlic and vinegar in a food processor or blender until smooth.

2. Add the oil, a few drops at a time, and when the mixture starts to thicken, add it in a thin continuous stream until all the oil has been used. Stir in the ground almonds and season with salt.

3. Spoon into a serving dish and serve with the lightly cooked vegetables.

INDEX

OTHER COOKBOOKS FROM THE CROSSING PRESS

The World in Your Kitchen
Vegetarian Recipes from Africa, Asia and Latin America
By Troth Wells
Foreword by Glenda Jackson
This is a delightful and diverse collection of 150 easy-to-cook vegetarian dishes
from around the world, fully adapted for the Western kitchen.
$16.95 • Paper • ISBN 0-89594-577-0

Mother Nature's Garden
Healthy Vegan Cooking
By Florence and Mickey Bienenfeld
In addition to eliminating animal products, including eggs and dairy, these 400
vegan recipes are low in fat and salt, cholesterol-free and sugar-free.
$14.95 • Paper • ISBN 0-89594-702-1

The Spice Box
Vegetarian Indian Cookbook
By Manju Shivraj Singh

115,063

"I strongly recommend *The Spice Box* . . . . Recipes for the most part are
simple and straightforward, but the end results would never reveal the
simplicity of the food's preparation." —*Vegetarian Times*
$12.95 • Paper • ISBN 0-89594-053-1

115,064

Japanese Vegetarian Cooking
From Simple Soups to Sushi
By Patricia Richfield
More than 100 vegetarian recipes, with easy-to-follow directions and information
on techniques, as well as a glossary of Japanese ingredients and utensils.
$14.95 • Paper • ISBN 0-89594-805-2

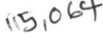

Low-Fat Vegetarian Cooking
Classic Slim Cuisine
By Sue Kreitzman
Adapting popular vegetarian dishes from the cuisines of the world, Master chef
Sue Kreitzman has created more than 100 new low-fat or non-fat dishes.
$14.95 • Paper • ISBN 0-89594-834-6

To receive a current catalog from
The Crossing Press
please call toll-free,
800-777-1048.